AQA Science

CW00531636

Revision Guide

David Brown • James Hayward • Jo Locke

Series Editor: Lawrie Ryan

GCSE Applied Science (Double Award)

Nelson Thornes

Published in 2006 by:
Nelson Thornes Ltd
Delta Place
27 Bath Road
CHELTENHAM
GL53 7TH
United Kingdom

08 09 10 / 10 9 8 7 6 5 4

A catalogue record for this book is available from the British Library

ISBN 978 0 7487 8320 5

Cover bubble illustration by Andy Parker
Cover photographs Oil rig/sun Photodisc 22 (NT); Radio telescopes/sun Photodisc 54 (NT);
Wheat/grass field Corel 227 (NT)
Illustrations by Oxford Designers and Illustrators, Peters and Zabransky and Roger Penwill

Page make-up by Design Practitioners Ltd

Printed in India by Replika Press Pvt. Ltd.

Photograph Acknowledgements:

Alamy: Adrian Sherrat p54(t); Beateworks Inc p57(b); Imagestate p61(b); Michael Riccio p60(r); Corel (NT): 48 p55(b); 437 p54(l), 681 p41, p75; 711 p57(tl); 714 p40; Digital Vision (NT): 6 p57(tr); Hart/Photodisc (NT): 24 p88; 50 p29; HMSO (Driving Standards Agency) p72; Ingram Pr V2 CD5 (NT) p54(r); Jim Breithaupt p61(t); Martyn Chillmaid p77(b); NASA p82(l); Photodisc (NT): 28 p63(t), p68(l); 46 p57(tc); 54 p80(l), p83; 75 p12; Roperhurst Ltd p56(b); Rubberball (NT) p55(t); Science Photo Library: Alex Bartel p 42; Alfred Pasieka p15(l); Andrew Lambert p56(t); Antonia Reeve p80(r); Cordelia Molloy p60(l); Curt Maas/Agstock p28; Dr Kari Lounatmaa p15(r); Gusto p88; Julian Baum/New Scientist p82(r); Paul Repson p77(t); SCIMAT p31; Sheila Terry p60(b); Steve Diamond p65, p67; Stockbyte (NT) 28 p54(c), p63(b), p68(r); Topfoto p51, p53

Additional picture research by SPL and Alison Prior

With thanks to Pauline Anning, Gerry Blake, Stewart Chenery and Kevin Ward.

Where?

Try to find somewhere quiet to work, away from the usual 'family noise'.

How?

- Use a range of techniques – some will work for you better than others.
- Using a variety of strategies will stop you getting 'bored'!

Kinaesthetic (doing)

- Make revision cards.
- Highlight key words.
- Plan ahead – make a revision timetable.
- Seek advice from teachers / friends.
- Make quizzes for classmates. Swap!

Visual (looking / drawing)

- Draw 'mind-maps'. Link together key ideas.
- Make big posters – especially of diagrams you might be asked to label.
- Use Post-it notes. Cover your bedroom furniture with key facts!
- Draw diagrams.

Auditory (speaking / listening)

- Discuss ideas with others.
- Say ideas out loud.
- Ask your teachers questions.
- Get family and friends to test you regularly.

How to Revise

Practise questions

- Attempt the **Pre Tests** before you start revising each chapter. These help you to find out how much you already know, and what you need to do some more work on.
- Answer the **Check yourself** questions as you revise to see how much you are learning.
- Answer the **Exam-style questions** to find out what will be expected in the exam itself, on pages 24, 44, 68 and 84.
- Check the **Examples of exam answers** to see where marks could be gained, on pages 25, 45, 67 and 85.
- Answer the **Final exam papers**, pages 86–8

See page 90 for answers.

How to answer questions

Question speak

Command word or phrase	What am I being asked to do?
compare	State the similarities and the differences between two or more things.
complete	Write words or numbers in the gaps provided.
describe	Use words and/or diagrams to say how something looks or how something happens.
draw	Make a drawing to show the important features of something.
draw a bar chart / graph	Use given data to draw a bar chart or plot a graph. For a graph, draw a line of best fit.
explain	Apply reasoning to account for the way something is or why something has happened. It is not enough to list reasons without discussing their relevance.
give / name / state	This only needs a short answer without explanation.
list	Write the information asked for in the form of a list.
predict	Say what you think will happen based on your knowledge and using information you may be given
sketch	A sketch requires less detail than a drawing but should be clear and concise. A sketch graph does not have to be drawn to scale but it should be the appropriate shape and have labelled axes.
suggest	There may be a variety of acceptable answers rather than one single answer. You may need to apply scientific knowledge and/or principles in an unfamiliar context.
use the information	Your answer must be based on information given in some form within the question.
what is meant by	You need to give a definition. You may also need to add some relevant comments.

How long should my answer be?

Things to consider:

1 How many lines have been given for the answer?
- One line suggests a single word or sentence. Several lines suggest a longer and more detailed answer is needed.

2 How many marks is the answer worth?
- There is usually one mark for each valid point so, for example, to get all of the marks available for a three mark question you will have to make three different, valid points.

3 As well as lines, is there also a blank space?
- Does the question require you to draw a diagram as part of your answer.
- You may have the option to draw a diagram as part of your answer.

Graphs

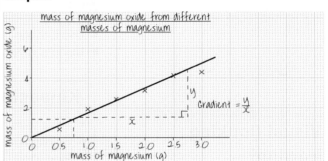

Things to remember:

- Choose sensible scales so the graph takes up most of the grid.
- Don't choose scales that will leave small squares equal to 3 as it is difficult to plot values with sufficient accuracy on such scales.
- Label the axes including units.
- Plot all points accurately by drawing small crosses using a fine pencil.
- Don't try to draw a line through every point. Draw a line of best fit.
- A line of best fit does not have to go through the origin.
- When drawing a line of best fit, don't include any points which obviously don't fit the pattern.
- The graph should have a title stating what it is.
- To find a corresponding value on the y-axis, draw a vertical line from the x-axis to the graph, and a horizontal line from the graph to the y-axis. Find a corresponding value on the x-axis in a similar way.
- The gradient or slope of a graph is the amount it changes on the y-axis divided by the amount it changes on the x-axis.

Diagrams

Ceramic wool soaked in medicinal paraffin
Delivery tube
Gaseous product
Broken pot (catalyst)
Heat
Water

Things to remember:

- Draw diagrams in pencil.
- The diagram needs to be large enough to see any important details.
- Light colouring could be used to improve clarity.
- The diagram should be fully labelled.
- Label lines should be thin and come from the point on the diagram that corresponds to the label.

Calculations

- Write down the equation you are going to use, if it is not already given.
- If you need to, rearrange the equation.
- Make sure that the quantities you put into the equation are in the right units, for example you may need to change centimetres to metres or grams to kilograms.
- Show the stages in your working. Even if your answer is wrong you can still gain method marks.
- If you have used a calculator make sure that your answer makes sense. Try doing the calculation in your head with rounded numbers.
- Give a unit with your final answer, if one is not already given.
- Be neat. Write numbers clearly. If the examiner cannot read what you have written your work will not gain credit. It may help to write a few words to explain what you have done.

Working with numbers in your exam

When you need to calculate answers, don't forget to:

- Remember your calculator!
- Set your workings out carefully.

Setting your workings out

There is a standard sequence you can follow that will help you to set your work out clearly. Here it is, with workings for an example question:

Question: A car is moving at 20 m/s. How far does it travel in 2 minutes?

What you should do	Full workings	Advice
1. Write down the equation.	Speed = distance ÷ time	Try to learn all of the equations you need to know.
2. Rearrange the equation if you need to.	Distance = speed × time	You should practise rearranging the common equations.
3. Put the numbers in – and watch out for conversions.	= 20 × (2 × 60)	The most common conversions are time and prefixes – e.g. minutes to seconds or kilowatts to watts.
4. Work out the answer (carefully).	= 2400	Compare your answer to an estimate to double check.
5. Add the units.	= 2400 m	Check the units given in the question.
6. Check that it is sensible.		This distance is just over 2 km – that's a sensible distance for a car to cover in 2 minutes.

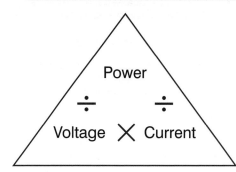

Rearranging equations

One way to learn equations is to put them into triangles like this one. Just cover the quantity you are trying to work out with a finger and it tells you what to do. For example, to work out current, cover it up and you are left with power ÷ voltage.

Averages

To work out an average, you add the numbers and divide by how many there are – just remember to press the $=$ button before the dividing.

Tables, graphs and charts

You need to be able to put information onto, as well as take information off these.

Whenever you see a table, graph or chart, *read it first* to see what it is about before reading the question.

Percentages

- Remember the rule:

$$\text{percentage} = \frac{\text{is}}{\text{of}} \times 100$$

- Use estimates to check that your answer is sensible (e.g. you can't get more than 100%).

Tick when you:

reviewed it after your lesson	✔	☐	☐
revised once – some questions right	✔	✔	☐
revised twice – all questions right	✔	✔	✔

Move onto another topic when you have all three ticks.

Section 1 Health and medicine

1.1 What are we made of?   ☐ ☐ ☐

1.2 What goes into and out of your cells?   ☐ ☐ ☐

1.3 How do your cells change food into energy?   ☐ ☐ ☐

1.4 Do all cells look the same?   ☐ ☐ ☐

1.5 How are substances transported around the body?   ☐ ☐ ☐

1.6 What happens when we breathe?   ☐ ☐ ☐

1.7 How do we react to changes in our environment?   ☐ ☐ ☐

1.8 Why do we have hormones?   ☐ ☐ ☐

1.9 How do we avoid getting too hot or too cold?   ☐ ☐ ☐

1.10 Why does everyone look different?   ☐ ☐ ☐

1.11 Why do we look like our parents?   ☐ ☐ ☐

1.12 Why don't we look identical to our parents?   ☐ ☐ ☐

1. **What is the function of chloroplasts in a plant cell?**

2. **How does oxygen move into cells from the blood?**

3. **What important energy producing process takes place inside your mitochondria?**

4. **Name three examples of specialised cells.**

5. **Why does the heart need to constantly pump blood around your body?**

6. **Which gases are exchanged in a cell?**

7. **Name the three types of neurone.**

8. **What are the main differences between a hormonal and nervous response?**

9. **How does sweating cool you down?**

10. **Name three human characteristics that are not affected by the environment.**

11. **What is the chemical called that contains all the information needed to make an organism?**

12. **What are alleles?**

1.1 What are we made of?

KEY POINTS

1 All living organisms are made up of tiny structures called **cells**.
2 The main features of animal cells are: a nucleus, cytoplasm and a cell membrane.
3 Plant cells contain these features and three important extra features – a cell wall, a vacuole and chloroplasts.

CHECK YOURSELF

1 What is the function of a nucleus?
2 Where in the cell does respiration occur?
3 Why do plant cells need a cell wall?

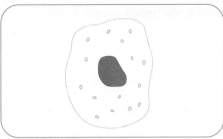

An animal cell

A plant cell

- **Cytoplasm** – This is a 'jelly-like' substance. All the chemical reactions in a cell take place here.
- **Cell membrane** – This is a barrier around the cell. It controls what can come in and out of the cell.
- **Nucleus** – This contains the information to decide what a cell will look like and what it does. It also contains the information needed to make new cells.

Plant cells also contain:

- **Cell wall** – This is made of cellulose. Cellulose is a tough fibre, which makes the wall rigid and supports the cell.
- **Vacuole** – This is full of a liquid called 'cell sap', a watery solution containing sugar and salts.
- **Chloroplasts** – These are green because they contain **chlorophyll**. The chlorophyll traps light energy needed for photosynthesis.

1.2 What goes into and out of your cells?

KEY POINTS

1 Substances move into and out of your cells by **diffusion**.
2 Water moves into and out of cells by **osmosis**. This is a special type of diffusion.

GET IT RIGHT!

Read the question carefully. If the question asks you to *explain* a process – do not just describe. You also need to say *why* things happen.

What is **diffusion**? It is the movement of particles *from* a place of high concentration *to* a place of low concentration. Diffusion takes place in all liquids and gases.

What is **osmosis**? Water molecules move *from* an area where they are in a high concentration *to* an area where they are in a low concentration, through a partially permeable membrane. The cell membrane is **partially permeable** – it contains tiny holes through which water molecules can move but larger molecules, like glucose, can't.

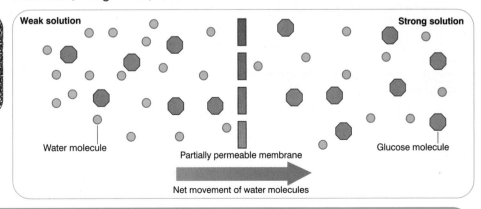

Water moves in and out of cells by osmosis

CHECK YOURSELF

1 What do we mean by 'a partially permeable membrane'?

2 What happens to particles during the process of diffusion?

1.3 How do your cells change food into energy?

KEY POINTS

1 Your cells convert food into energy by the process of respiration.
2 During this process, oxygen is used up and the waste products carbon dioxide and water are produced.
3 Respiration takes place inside your mitochondria.

Your body needs energy to do everything – like moving, growing and staying warm. We get energy from our food. But to release energy, food has to be 'burned' in oxygen. This reaction is called **aerobic respiration**.

$$\text{glucose} + \text{oxygen} \rightarrow \text{carbon dioxide} + \text{water} + \textbf{energy}$$

$$C_6H_{12}O_6 + 6O_2 \rightarrow 6CO_2 + 6H_2O + \textbf{energy}$$

Respiration happens inside tiny structures inside your cells called **mitochondria**.

Your rate of respiration can be measured with a respirometer. This measures how quickly a person uses up oxygen.

GET IT RIGHT!

Don't forget that breathing and respiration are *not* the same thing!
● Breathing is taking in and removing air from your lungs.
● Respiration is the process of releasing energy from your food.

EXAM HINTS

Note how you need to write an answer. For example, if the question says 'Give the word equation for respiration.', write your answer in words e.g. 'oxygen' *not* 'O₂'.

CHECK YOURSELF

1 Write the word equation that summarises respiration.

2 Why are there lots of mitochondria in your muscle cells?

1.4 Do all cells look the same?

KEY POINTS

1 Specialised cells perform specific roles in plants and animals. You can often tell what a cell does by its appearance.
2 Specialised animal cells include red blood cells, white blood cells and nerve cells.
3 Specialised plant cells include root hair cells and leaf palisade cells.

Not all cells in your body or in a plant look the same. Cells have different jobs to do and this affects their design. These cells are called **specialised cells**.

Here are three examples of specialised animal cells:

Red blood cells – their job is to carry oxygen around the body.

● They are small and have no nucleus.
● They are a disc-like shape to increase the surface area for carrying oxygen.
● They contain **haemoglobin** (a red pigment).

A red blood cell

White blood cells – their job is to fight disease.

● They are large and have a nucleus.
● They can change shape so the cell can **engulf pathogens**.

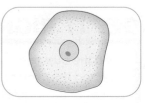

A white blood cell

Nerve cells – their job is to transmit electrical impulses around the body.

● They are long and thin.
● They are covered in fat, to insulate the body from the impulse and prevent the message being scrambled.
● They have receptors to detect stimuli like light and sound.

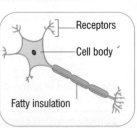

Receptors

Cell body

Fatty insulation

A nerve cell

EXAM HINTS

Read the question carefully. If the question asks you to 'describe', write *what happens* (for a process, e.g. photosynthesis), or *list the features* (for a structure).

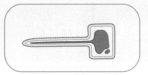

A root hair cell

A leaf palisade cell

Here are two examples of specialised plant cells:

Root hair cells – their job is to absorb water and nutrients from the soil.

- They have a root hair, giving a large surface area for absorbing water.
- They have no chloroplasts, as there is no light underground!

Leaf palisade cells – these are the main sites of photosynthesis.

- They are long and thin, giving a large surface area for absorbing light.
- They contain lots of chloroplasts for photosynthesis.

students' book
page 40

1.5

How are substances transported around the body?

KEY POINTS

1 The heart is a muscle, which pumps blood around the body, supplying the cells with oxygen.

2 Blood is made up of red blood cells, white blood cells, platelets and plasma.

3 Blood travels in vessels around the body. There are three types – arteries, capillaries and veins.

The **heart** is a muscle, which constantly pumps blood around the body. It delivers oxygen and nutrients to the cells and removes waste.

Blood is made up of:

- **Red blood cells** – they carry oxygen.
- **White blood cells** – they fight disease by engulfing microbes and making antibodies.
- **Plasma** – it carries digested food, waste such as carbon dioxide, hormones, blood cells and antibodies. It is a straw-coloured liquid and mainly contains water.
- **Platelets** – they help the blood to **clot**. These are fragments of cells.

Blood travels around your body in **blood vessels**. There are three types:

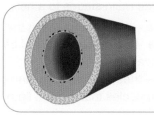

An **artery** carries blood away from the heart under high pressure

Veins return blood to the heart. They have valves to stop blood flowing backwards

Capillaries are tiny vessels. The wall is only 1 cell thick, so substances can easily move through them

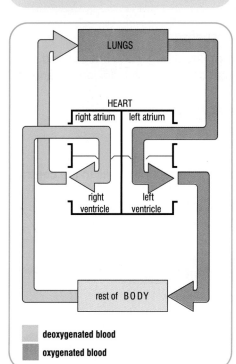

deoxygenated blood
oxygenated blood

How the heart circulates blood through the body. Blood flows through the heart twice during each circuit of the body. It is called a 'double circulatory system'

1.6 What happens when we breathe?

- You breathe in oxygen and breathe out carbon dioxide. This process is called **gas exchange**.
- **Inhaling** – Your intercostal muscles *contract* (pulling your rib-cage up and out) and your diaphragm *contracts* (moves down). This *increases* the volume of your thorax. The pressure in the thorax *decreases* and air is drawn *in*.
- **Exhaling** – Your intercostal muscles *relax* (lowering your rib-cage) and your diaphragm *relaxes* (moves up). This *decreases* the volume of your thorax. The pressure in the thorax *increases* and air is forced *out*.
- Your lungs are found inside your **thorax**, and are protected by your rib-cage. Below the lungs there is a large sheet of muscle called the **diaphragm**. This separates the thorax from the abdomen below.

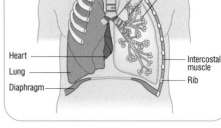

The inside of the thorax

1.7 How do we react to changes in our environment?

There are three main stages to a nervous response:

- **A stimulus** – this is a change in the environment, e.g. light, heat, sound.
- **Receptors** – these are groups of cells that detect the stimulus and change it into electrical impulses.
- **Effectors** – these are muscles and glands that cause a response, for example, muscles that move a limb.

There are three types of neurone:

- **Sensory neurones** – they carry messages from receptor cells to the **central nervous system (CNS)**.
- **Relay neurones** – they connect sensory neurones to motor neurones.
- **Motor neurones** – they carry messages from the CNS to effectors.

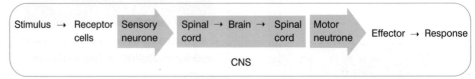

The steps involved in a normal nervous response – a controlled reaction

1.8 Why do we have hormones?

1 Hormones are chemical messengers, which are produced by **glands**. They travel in the blood to **target cells** where they cause a response.
2 Insulin is a hormone produced by the pancreas. It is involved in controlling blood sugar levels. If you cannot make enough insulin you suffer from the disease diabetes.

CHECK YOURSELF

1 Name three examples of hormones.

2 Where are hormones made?

- Hormones control body processes that need constant adjustment – such as body temperature. Keeping a constant internal environment is called **homeostasis**.

Hormones and nerves carry out similar roles but act in very different ways:

	Nerves	Hormones
Speed of response	Very fast	Slower
Length of response	Short acting	Longer acting
Area targeted	Very precise area	Larger area
Time of reaction	Immediate	Longer term

Controlling blood sugar levels

After eating, your blood sugar level rises. If this stays high it is dangerous. Pancreas cells detect high blood sugar levels, and release **insulin**. Insulin tells the liver to store **glucose** by converting it into **glycogen**. As glucose is removed from the blood, the blood sugar level falls. If the blood glucose level is too low, insulin is not released. The liver now turns glycogen back into glucose, which raises the blood sugar level.

Diabetics do not produce enough insulin. This means that their blood sugar levels can rise to fatal levels. Diabetics have to avoid eating large quantities of carbohydrate-rich foods. In more severe cases they have to inject themselves with insulin.

1.9 How do we avoid getting too hot or too cold?

1 To work efficiently your body needs to maintain a temperature of 37°C. Changes in your skin help to maintain this temperature.
2 These include the production of sweat, changes in the diameter of blood capillaries, movement of hairs and shivering.

CHECK YOURSELF

1 At what temperature does your body work most efficiently?

2 Name three changes that take place in your skin when you get too hot.

3 How does shivering raise your body temperature?

Your body works best at 37°C. Your brain monitors blood temperature and skin receptor cells receive information about the external temperature. The brain processes this information, and sends messages to tell the body how to respond.

What happens when you get too hot?

- Hairs on your skin lie flat.
- Sweat glands produce sweat. Sweat is mainly water, but also contains salt and urea (a waste material). The water evaporates from the surface of your skin. As it evaporates it takes heat energy from the body, making you feel cooler.
- Blood vessels (capillaries) near the surface of your skin widen (**vasodilation**). This allows more blood to flow close to the surface of the skin. So more heat is lost from the blood by radiation, cooling you down.

What happens when you get too cold?

- Hairs on your skin stand on end – this traps a layer of air close to the skin, preventing heat loss.
- Sweat glands do not produce sweat.
- Blood vessels near the surface of your skin narrow (**vasoconstriction**).
- Shivering (rapid muscle contractions) – this requires extra energy, so your cells respire more producing extra heat.

1.10 Why does everyone look different?

GET IT RIGHT!

Make sure you know what the words 'environmental' and 'genetic' variation mean, and some examples of characteristics influenced by each. Remember that many characteristics (e.g. height) show both environmental and genetic variation.

Differences within members of a species are called **variation**. People vary in many different **characteristics** including height, build, hair colour and intelligence.

There are two factors that cause variation:

● the characteristics you inherit from your parents – **genetic variation**
● the environment in which you live – **environmental variation**.

Most characteristics are affected by both environmental and genetic variation, for example hair colour. At birth this characteristic shows genetic variation – people generally have the same colour hair as one of their parents. However this person's blue and spiky hair is an example of environmental variation. The person has chosen to dye and style their hair in this way.

In humans there are many characteristics that are not influenced by the environment. Examples include eye colour, natural hair colour, blood group, and the presence of a genetic disorder (like cystic fibrosis or haemophilia).

CHECK YOURSELF

1 What do we mean by the term 'variation'?
2 Name three examples of human characteristics.
3 Does height show genetic or environmental variation? Explain.

1.11 Why do we look like our parents?

GET IT RIGHT!

You must learn the definitions of these key words: DNA, gene, chromosome and nucleus.

You **inherit** characteristics from your parents through genetic material. Inside the **nucleus** of your cells are **chromosomes**. These are strands of the chemical **DNA**, which contain all the information needed to make a human being.

Each chromosome is divided into sections of DNA. Each contains the information needed to produce a single characteristic like eye or hair colour. These coding sections are called **genes**. One chromosome contains thousands of genes.

Inside the nucleus of your normal body cells are 23 pairs of chromosomes (so 46 altogether). One of each pair comes from your mother. The other comes from your father. Egg and sperm cells are the only cells in the body to contain just 23 chromosomes.

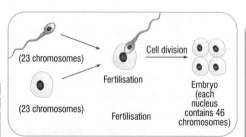

During fertilisation genetic material from the egg and sperm combine

CHECK YOURSELF

1 How many chromosomes are found in a sperm cell?
2 How many chromosomes are found in a skin cell?
3 What is a gene?

1.12 Why don't we look identical to our parents?

KEY POINTS

1 Different forms of the same gene are called **alleles**.
2 There are two main types of allele: **dominant** genes, which are always expressed if present in a nucleus, and **recessive** genes.
3 Recessive genes will only be expressed if you have two copies of them.

AQA EXAMINER SAYS...

To ensure that you get top marks on a genetic cross question, write the cross out in full to make sure that you don't make a simple mistake. Follow the steps in the diagram on this page carefully.

You have two genes for each characteristic – one from your mother and one from your father. These two genes may be the same, but they may be different. Different forms of the same gene are called **alleles**.

- Some genes will always be **expressed** – these are called **dominant** genes (for example, the gene that codes for black hair).
- Weaker genes, like the blonde hair gene, are called **recessive** genes. Recessive genes will only be expressed if you have two copies of them.

Dominant genes are always represented in genetic crosses with a capital letter. For eye colour, brown eyes are dominant and blue eyes are recessive:

Mother – blue eyes **bb**   **BB** brown eyes – **Father**

Eggs contain   b   b   B   B   Sperm contain

	B	B
b	Bb	Bb
b	Bb	Bb

All children will have the genes **Bb**. This means that they will have brown eyes, as this is the dominant gene.

CHECK YOURSELF

1 What is the difference between a recessive and a dominant gene?
2 Name some alleles of the hair colour gene.

Chapter 1 — End of chapter questions

1 Name the four main features of an animal cell.

2 What type of molecules move into and out of cells by osmosis?

3 Which two waste products are produced as a result of respiration?

4 What is a specialised cell?

5 Name the three types of blood vessel found in your body.

6 How do the structures inside your thorax move to allow you to breathe in?

7 Describe the steps involved in a nervous response.

8 What is the role of insulin in the body?

9 Name three changes that take place in your skin when you are too cold.

10 Name three bird characteristics that show variation.

11 How is genetic material passed from a father to his child?

12 If a woman with blonde hair and a man with black hair have a child, what colour hair is the child likely to have?

Chapter 2 — Checklist: Unhealthy body

Tick when you:

reviewed it after your lesson	✓	☐	☐
revised once – some questions right	✓	✓	☐
revised twice – all questions right	✓	✓	✓

Move onto another topic when you have all three ticks.

Section 1 Health and medicine

2.1 What are harmful microorganisms? ☐ ☐ ☐

2.2 How are diseases spread? ☐ ☐ ☐

2.3 How are microorganisms stopped from harming us? ☐ ☐ ☐

2.4 What makes a healthy diet? ☐ ☐ ☐

2.5 How can drugs harm your body? ☐ ☐ ☐

2.6 How does smoking tobacco harm your body? ☐ ☐ ☐

2.7 How does drinking alcohol affect us? ☐ ☐ ☐

2.8 Genetically inherited disorders ☐ ☐ ☐

Chapter 2 — Pre Test: Unhealthy body

1. How could you tell the difference between a bacteria and a virus?

2. How could you protect yourself from catching (a) a cold, (b) chicken pox?

3. How do lymphocytes protect you from disease?

4. Why is protein important in your diet?

5. Name two examples of legal and illegal drugs.

6. How is carbon monoxide harmful to the body?

7. What is the name of the drug found in alcoholic drinks?

8. Name two examples of inherited disorders.

2.1 What are harmful microorganisms?

Microorganisms are living things, at least 100 times smaller than your cells. Most cause no harm to animals or plants, but some can cause disease. These are called **pathogens**.

KEY POINTS

1 Microorganisms are tiny living organisms. Some can be beneficial but others can cause disease.
2 There are three types of microorganism: bacteria, viruses and fungi.
3 Both bacteria and viruses can cause disease by damaging your cells.
4 Bacteria replicate by dividing in two, but viruses have to use your cells to reproduce.

Microorganism	Bacterium	Virus
Appearance		
Features	<ul><li>Cell wall</li><li>No nucleus</li><li>Genetic material floats around in the cytoplasm</li></ul>	<ul><li>Have a protein coat</li><li>No nucleus</li><li>A few genes, which float inside the virus</li><li>Smaller than bacteria</li></ul>
Diseases caused	<ul><li>Tuberculosis</li><li>Salmonella</li><li>Pneumonia</li></ul>	<ul><li>Measles</li><li>Rubella</li><li>Flu</li></ul>
How they cause disease	By damaging cells or producing **toxins**	By damaging cells
How they replicate	In good conditions they divide into two every 20 minutes	Using your cells

CHECK YOURSELF

1 Name two diseases caused by a bacterium and two diseases caused by a virus.

2 How do bacteria replicate?

3 How do viruses cause disease?

BUMP UP YOUR GRADE

You may be asked to read information off microbial growth charts. When you take a reading from a graph, you should use a pencil and ruler to read off the numbers, so it is clear to the examiner how you reached your answer. See the diagram.

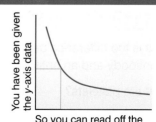

So you can read off the value on the x-axis which goes with it

How are diseases spread?

Pathogens can enter our bodies through:

- cuts in the skin
- the digestive, respiratory and reproductive systems
- animal bites.

How can you protect yourself catching a disease from an infected person?

Protection method	Protected against	Method of spread
Covering your mouth and nose e.g. using a mask or handkerchief	Colds and flu	When somebody sneezes or coughs tiny drops of liquid are released into the air – **droplet infection**
Not touching infected people or objects they have contaminated	Mumps and chicken pox	Some diseases are **contagious**. They are spread by touching infected people and in some cases touching objects an infected person has touched
Using condoms	Syphilis and gonorrhoea plus HIV and hepatitis	Through body fluids exchanged during sexual intercourse
Using new sterilised needles and disposing of old needles carefully	HIV and hepatitis	Through blood

How are microorganisms stopped from harming us?

If your skin is damaged, e.g. cut or grazed, pathogens can enter the body. The skin therefore needs to seal a cut as quickly as possible. This also stops you losing too much blood.

If microorganisms do enter the body, white blood cells prevent them causing disease. There are two types of white blood cell:

- **Lymphocytes** – they detect that something 'foreign' has entered your body. They then make an **antibody** to attack the microorganism. Each antibody is specific for one type of microorganism. Every time a new microorganism enters the body, a new antibody needs to be made.

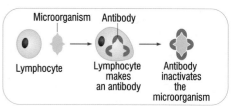

Lymphocyte attacking a microorganism

After they have fought the disease, some antibodies remain in your blood to prevent you getting the disease again. This provides you with **immunity**.

Lymphocytes also make **anti-toxins**. These chemicals destroy poisonous toxins that some microorganisms make.

- **Phagocytes** – they **engulf** (swallow) microorganisms. They then make enzymes, which digest the microorganism.

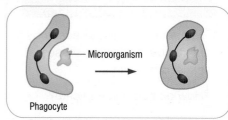

Phagocyte attacking a microorganism

2.4 What makes a healthy diet?

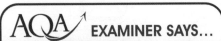

EXAMINER SAYS…

Questions relating to balanced diets and food groups are very common. Know the main food groups, their role in the body, and examples of foods that contain them.

Food group	Role in the body	Examples of food
Carbohydrates	Main source of energy	Pasta, rice, bread
Proteins	Building and repairing cells	Fish, eggs, meat
Fats	Store of energy, keep you warm and cover your vital organs, protecting them from damage	Butter, cheese, red meat
Vitamins and minerals	Needed in small quantities to keep you healthy	Fruit, vegetables
Fibre	Is not digested, but adds bulk to your food so that waste can be pushed out of the digestive system more easily. Fibre also absorbs poisonous waste made when you digest food	Cereal, vegetables
Water	Makes up two-thirds of your body. All cell reactions take place in water and substances have to dissolve in it to be carried around the blood	Water

To stay healthy you need to eat a **balanced diet**. If you eat too much food the body will store it as fat. Over time you may become overweight and eventually obese. This increases your risk of heart disease, diabetes, some cancers and gout. If you eat too little food, then you will become weak and have little energy to do anything.

There are two types of fat – saturated (animal origin) and unsaturated (plant origin). If you eat too much saturated fat, it sticks to the lining of your blood vessels. This makes them narrower. Your heart has to work harder to pump the blood through these vessels, increasing your risk of a heart attack.

CHECK YOURSELF

1 Name some examples of foods that contain carbohydrates.
2 Why do you need to eat?
3 What is the difference between saturated fat and unsaturated fat?

2.5 How can drugs harm your body?

CHECK YOURSELF

1 How does a drug cause its effect?
2 What is the difference between a drug that is a stimulant and one that is a depressant?

Drugs are chemicals that affect the way your body works. They alter the chemical reactions that take place inside your body. If your body gets used to these changes it may become **dependent** on a drug. If this happens you are **addicted**. When an addict stops taking the drug, they suffer **withdrawal symptoms**.

These are **legal drugs**:
- Alcohol – this affects your nervous system and damages your liver.
- Tobacco – this increases your risk of cancer, respiratory and heart disease.
- Anti-depressants – these relieve depression. However, prolonged use can lead to addiction.

Illegal drugs – These can kill or damage your body, even in very small amounts:

Drug	How it affects the body	Harmful effect on the body
Barbiturates	Depressants – slow down the nervous system	Hallucinations, heart attack
Heroin		Addictive, risk of coma
Amphetamines	Stimulants – speed up the nervous system	Addictive, memory loss
Cocaine		Aggression, brain damage

How does smoking tobacco harm your body?

1 Smoking tobacco significantly increases your risk of suffering from heart disease, lung cancer and respiratory disorders like emphysema and bronchitis.
2 Tobacco smoke has three main components: tar (causes cancer), nicotine (is addictive) and carbon monoxide (reduces the oxygen carrying capacity of the blood).

BUMP UP YOUR GRADE

When you are asked to explain how smoking affects the body, higher level answers *not* only list the health problems caused by smoking, but also explain how the problem is caused.

Tobacco smoke contains over a thousand chemicals, many of which are harmful:

- **Tar** – this collects in the lungs when the smoke cools. It is a sticky black material that irritates and narrows your airways. Some of the chemicals it contains cause **cancer**.
- **Nicotine** – this is addictive. It affects the nervous system, makes the heart beat faster and narrows blood vessels. Narrow blood vessels easily become blocked and lead to heart attacks and strokes.
- **Carbon monoxide** – this is a poisonous gas. It stops the red blood cells from carrying as much oxygen as they should, by binding to haemoglobin in the place of oxygen.

Chemicals in tobacco smoke cause alveoli walls to weaken and lose their flexibility. They do not inflate properly and can burst during coughing. Not enough oxygen passes into the blood, leaving the person breathless. This disease is called **emphysema**.

Chemicals in tobacco smoke also paralyse the cilia on the cells lining your windpipe. Mucus now flows into your lungs, making it hard to breathe and often causes infection – **bronchitis**. Smokers have to cough this mucus up, damaging their lungs further.

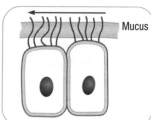

Mucus

A ciliated cell. The cells in your windpipe make mucus. This traps dirt and microorganisms. The tiny hairs (cilia) move mucus along to keep your airways clean.

CHECK YOURSELF

1 What are the three main components of tobacco smoke?
2 How does nicotine harm the body?
3 How does smoking damage the ciliated cells which line your windpipe?

How does drinking alcohol affect us?

1 Alcohol contains the drug ethanol that affects your nervous system and changes your behaviour.
2 Long term drinking can cause heart disease, brain damage and sclerosis of the liver.

CHECK YOURSELF

1 Which organ in the body breaks down alcohol?
2 Approximately how long would it take your body to break down six units of alcohol?

Alcoholic drinks contain the drug **ethanol**. It is a depressant, and even in small quantities can change your behaviour. Most people feel relaxed and happy but some become aggressive and depressed.

Alcohol is absorbed into your bloodstream in your intestines. It then travels to the brain where it affects your nervous system. Alcohol can affect the body for several hours – it takes about an hour for the body to break down one unit of alcohol ($\frac{1}{2}$ pint of beer).

Long term heavy drinking can cause stomach ulcers, heart disease and brain and liver damage. The liver breaks down ethanol (poisonous to the body) into harmless waste products. The livers of heavy drinkers become scarred – healthy cells are replaced with fat or fibrous tissue. The liver now performs less efficiently. This condition is known as **sclerosis** of the liver, and can be fatal.

People who drink alcohol regularly need greater and greater amounts to have the same effect on their body. This is because their body has developed a tolerance to ethanol. If they continue drinking they may become addicted – an alcoholic.

2.8 Genetically inherited disorders

Inherited disorders are passed on from parents to their children in their genes. Examples include cystic fibrosis and haemophilia.

Cystic fibrosis

- Cystic fibrosis is caused by a 'faulty' gene.
- A sufferer produces thick sticky mucus which blocks their air passages, making breathing difficult and often causing chest infections.
- Physiotherapy and antibiotics can help treat the symptoms, but there is no cure.
- Cystic fibrosis is caused by a recessive allele (represented by c), so a person only suffers from the disease if both their copies of the gene are 'faulty' (cc).
- People can be **carriers** of cystic fibrosis (Cc), i.e. they are healthy but can pass the disorder onto their children.

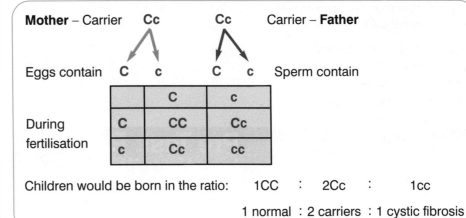

Mother – Carrier **Cc**   **Cc**   Carrier – **Father**

Eggs contain C   c   C   c   Sperm contain

	C	c
C	CC	Cc
c	Cc	cc

During fertilisation

Children would be born in the ratio: 1CC : 2Cc : 1cc

1 normal : 2 carriers : 1 cystic fibrosis

The diagram shows how two cystic fibrosis carriers can produce a child who suffers with the disease

CHECK YOURSELF

1 What are the symptoms of cystic fibrosis?

2 What is a 'carrier'?

Chapter 2   End of chapter questions

1 **How do viruses multiply?**

2 **Why is it important that you eat some fat in your diet?**

3 **What is a drug addict?**

4 **How does smoking increase your risk of emphysema?**

5 **How can alcohol damage the body?**

6 **What is meant by the term a 'sex-linked' inherited disease?**

Tick when you:

reviewed it after your lesson	☑	☐	☐
revised once – some questions right	☑	☑	☐
revised twice – all questions right	☑	☑	☑

Move onto another topic when you have all three ticks.

Section 1 Health and medicine

3.1	What can doctors prescribe to help us feel better?	☐	☐	☐
3.2	Protecting ourselves from harmful pathogens	☐	☐	☐
3.3	Immunisation	☐	☐	☐
3.4	How do X-rays diagnose medical conditions?	☐	☐	☐
3.5	What is radioactivity?	☐	☐	☐
3.6	Uses of ionising radiation	☐	☐	☐

| Chapter 3 | Pre Test: Preventing, diagnosing and treating illnesses |

1. How do antibiotics treat illnesses?

2. Name some steps that you should take to maintain your personal hygiene.

3. What do vaccines contain?

4. What are X-rays?

5. Name the three types of ionising radiation.

6. How does a tracer allow doctors to diagnose some medical conditions?

What can doctors prescribe to help us feel better?

 EXAMINER SAYS…

Make sure that you know how anti-inflammatory and antibiotic drugs work, and some examples of conditions that can be treated by each one.

Doctors can prescribe drugs to make you feel better. Some drugs work by killing the pathogen that has made you ill. Others work by relieving the symptoms of an illness.

- Penicillin is an **antibiotic**. These are drugs that kill bacteria but do not damage the cells in your body. They have no effect on viruses or fungi. There are several different types of antibiotic; each kills different species of bacteria.
- Aspirin and paracetamol treat the symptoms of a disease, but do not kill pathogens. Aspirins are **anti-inflammatory**. They reduce the swelling, which in turn stops pain. When you hurt yourself, the body releases prostaglandin. This makes you feel pain. Paracetamol reduces the production of this chemical, decreasing the pain that you feel.

CHECK YOURSELF

1 Can antibiotics be used to treat flu – a viral illness?

2 How does an anti-inflammatory drug work?

Protecting ourselves from harmful pathogens

You come into contact daily with potentially harmful microorganisms. To protect yourself from disease you should maintain your personal hygiene, e.g. wash your hands regularly, shower daily and clean your teeth twice a day. People working in the food industry have to wear special clothing (such as hats, gloves and coats) to stop them contaminating food.

Chemicals can be used to kill microorganisms. There are two main groups:
- **Antiseptics** – these kill microorganisms but do not damage your skin. For example, they are used to clean cuts.
- **Disinfectants** – they are much stronger chemicals and are therefore more effective at killing microorganisms. However they can damage skin cells, so must not be used on your skin. They are widely used to clean kitchens and toilets.

Sterilisation kills all microorganisms. **Sterile** objects have no microorganisms on them. Objects are usually sterilised with heat or radiation, although chemicals can be used.

GET IT RIGHT!

You need to know what the difference is between an antiseptic and a disinfectant. DisinfecTANTS are irriTANTS – so you would not use them on your skin!

CHECK YOURSELF

1 Name some areas where disinfectants should be used.

2 What is meant by a 'sterile' environment?

3.3 Immunisation

1 Immunisations protect you from diseases caused by microorganisms.
2 Dead or weakened microorganisms are used to trigger a response by your white blood cells.
3 The antibodies they produce remain in your body providing you with immunity against a disease.

CHECK YOURSELF

1 Name three common immunisations children receive.

2 Which immunisation is normally given by mouth rather than by injection?

Immunisation protects you from some diseases caused by microorganisms.

Most **vaccines** contain dead or weakened microorgansims that can no longer cause disease:

● These microorgansims do not make you ill, but still trigger your white blood cells to make antibodies.
● These antibodies destroy the microorganisms.
● Some remain in your body and will fight the microorganism off quickly if it enters your body again, preventing it causing disease. You now have **immunity** to the disease.

Three immunisations most children receive include:

● **Polio** (normally given by mouth) – Polio affects your nervous system and can lead to permanent paralysis and even death.
● **BCG** – This protects you against tuberculosis, which affects your lungs and causes breathing problems. In very severe cases it can cause death.
● **MMR** – This protects you from measles, mumps and rubella. As well as being unpleasant measles can cause deafness. Mumps can make men infertile. In extreme cases both diseases can be fatal. If a pregnant woman contracts rubella, the unborn baby may be born deaf, blind, or even die.

3.4 How do X-rays diagnose medical conditions?

1 X-rays are electromagnetic waves.
2 They are used to take images of dense structures (e.g. bones) inside the body.
3 High doses of X-rays can be dangerous, but people who work with X-rays are protected by using lead screens.

BUMP UP YOUR GRADE

Learn how an X-ray image is produced by using a bullet point list, or a flow chart. You can then use this if you are asked to explain how an X-ray image is made. Make sure the number of steps in your answer matches the number of marks available.

X-rays are high energy **waves**, which can ionise cells and cause cancer if high enough doses are received. They are just a small part of a large family of waves known as the **electromagnetic spectrum**.

X-ray images are produced in the following way:

● Photographic film is placed behind the patient.
● The patient is exposed to X-rays.
● X-rays penetrate through soft tissues like skin and muscle. They are absorbed by denser structures, such as bones and teeth.
● The X-rays that penetrate through the patient expose the film.
● The image is then developed. Regions that were exposed to X-rays show up black. Areas that were not exposed to X-rays are white.
● These images are known as 'shadow pictures'.

Radiographers are at risk of receiving high doses of X-radiation, so a lead screen (because it is very dense and absorbs X-rays), is placed between the radiographer and the patient. Radiographers also wear film badges, to measure the dose of radiation received.

CHECK YOURSELF

1 Why can X-rays pass through muscle but not bone?

2 Why can X-rays be said to be both damaging and beneficial to health?

3.5 What is radioactivity?

KEY POINTS

1 Atoms with unstable nuclei are radioactive – this means they emit ionising radiation.
2 Three types of ionising radiation exist: alpha, beta and gamma radiation.
3 All these types of radiation are harmful to humans, and can cause cancer if a large enough dose of the radiation is received.

GET IT RIGHT!

Don't confuse alpha and beta radiation (made of particles) with gamma radiation (made of high energy waves).

Some atoms have an unstable nucleus. They throw out particles and/or high energy waves. This process is known as **radioactivity**. The particles or rays that are emitted are known as **ionising radiation**. Any exposure to ionising radiation is potentially harmful. The greater the **dose** of radiation you receive, the greater the risk of cancer. People who work with radioactive substances minimise their radiation dose by:

- Ensuring they handle substances safely.
- Using shielding around the radioactive substances.
- Keeping their exposure times low (checked using a film badge).

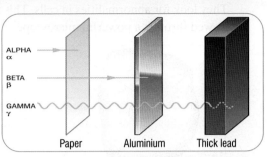
Diagram showing alpha, beta and gamma absorption

CHECK YOURSELF

1 For each type of radiation, suggest a material that could be used to absorb the radioactivity.
2 State four practices used by people who work with radioactive materials, to ensure that their exposure to radiation is as low as possible.

3.6 Uses of ionising radiation

KEY POINT

Radioactive materials can be used as tracers, to treat some illnesses, and to sterilise medical equipment. The type of radiation used for a particular job is chosen depending on its properties.

Radioactive tracers can be used to identify some medical disorders. Tracers (usually low energy gamma emitters) are swallowed, or injected into the patient. The radiation is then detected outside the body using a **gamma camera**.

Radiotherapy – This can be used to treat some forms of cancer. Gamma radiation is placed outside the body, and aimed at the tumour (although sometimes a radioactive **implant** is placed inside the tumour).

High doses of this radiation kills cancerous cells, but also damages some healthy cells around the cancer. This treatment can leave the patient feeling very ill.

CHECK YOURSELF

1 Name a use of radioactive tracers.
2 Describe how radioactive materials can be used to sterilise medical equipment.

Chapter 3 — End of chapter questions

1 **How does taking paracetamol reduce pain?**
2 **What is the difference between an antiseptic and a disinfectant?**
3 **How do immunisations cause immunity?**
4 **Why do radiographers work behind lead screens?**
5 **How can radioactive substances be used to treat some cancers?**

1 (a) Pathologists are scientists who work in hospitals. They look for abnormalities in cells. This is a cell viewed through a powerful microscope.

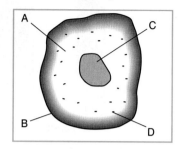

What type of cell are they looking at? (1 mark)

(b) Label the parts of the cell on the diagram, A–D, by using the words below. (4 marks)

cytoplasm   nucleus   cell membrane   mitochondria

(c) Match the parts of the cell with their functions in the body. (4 marks)

Cell feature	Function
Cytoplasm	A barrier that controls what comes into and out of the cell
Nucleus	Respiration takes place here. Glucose and oxygen react and release energy
Cell membrane	Contains the information needed to make new cells
Mitochondria	A 'jelly-like' substance where all the chemical reactions take place

(d) If a scientist were looking at a plant cell, what three extra features would they expect to see? (3 marks)

2 (a) To monitor an athlete's fitness levels, trainers often measure their rate of respiration.
Where does respiration take place? Choose the correct answer from these: (1 mark)
   In your chloroplasts
   In the nucleus
   In your mitochondria

(b) Respiration can be summarised using the following chemical equation:

$C_6H_{12}O_6 + 6O_2 \rightarrow 6CO_2 + 6H_2O$ + energy

Fill in the gaps in the word equation below: (2 marks)

glucose + ... $\rightarrow$ carbon dioxide + ... + energy

(c) Choose two foods from the list below that would provide you with a good source of glucose. (1 mark)

cheese   sugar   fish   milk   pasta   water

(d) By which process does the glucose needed for respiration move from your blood into your cells? (1 mark)

3 (a) Complete the following table using **X-rays**, **gamma rays**, **alpha particles** or **beta particles**. The words can be used once, more than once or not at all. (4 marks)

Ionising radiation used	Use of ionising radiation
	Sterilising medical equipment
	As an implant to treat a cancerous tumour
	Taking a shadow picture of a skeleton
	As a tracer to monitor blood flow around the body

(b) State one other example of how radioactive tracers can be used in the human body. (1 mark)

(c) Radiographers take several X-rays of patients each day. State one precaution a radiographer would take to ensure their received dose of radiation remains as low as possible. (1 mark)

(d) For your answer to part (c), explain how this precaution keeps the received dose as low as possible. (2 marks)

4 (a) A couple who are planning to have a baby visit a genetic counsellor to work out the likelihood of their child having cystic fibrosis. Name another example of an inherited disorder. (1 mark)

(b) Lucy does not display any symptoms of cystic fibrosis but she carries one copy of the 'faulty' cystic fibrosis gene. What is the scientific term for a person like this? (1 mark)

(c) To suffer from cystic fibrosis you have to have two copies of the faulty gene. Is cystic fibrosis a recessive or dominant disorder? (1 mark)

(d) If Lucy and Peter (also a cystic fibrosis carrier) have a child, what is the likelihood of their child being born with cystic fibrosis? Draw out a genetic cross to show how you arrive at your answer. (4 marks)

 Test & Assessment Interactive quizzes, answers and hints online!

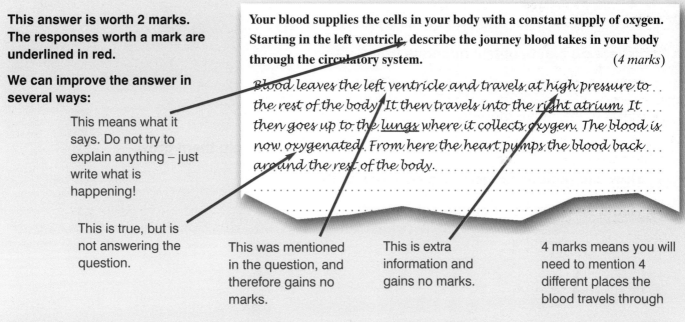

This is an excellent graph, and would score all 5 marks.

Points plotted correctly and accurately. (1 mark) (Remember to use a *sharp* pencil, and make a small cross where the point is plotted.)

Axes are labelled correctly, and with units. (1 mark)

The scale is linear (it changes by a set amount), even though the data in the table they were provided with did not. (1 mark)

In this question the student was given the data to draw the graph shown here. The question was worth 5 marks.

A line of best fit has been added (1 mark). This could be straight (as in this case), or curved, but should be smooth and go through as many of the points as possible.

The scale has been chosen to fit onto the graph paper provided as closely as possible. (1 mark)

This answer is worth 2 marks. The responses worth a mark are underlined in red.

We can improve the answer in several ways:

This means what it says. Do not try to explain anything – just write what is happening!

This is true, but is not answering the question.

This was mentioned in the question, and therefore gains no marks.

This is extra information and gains no marks.

4 marks means you will need to mention 4 different places the blood travels through

Your blood supplies the cells in your body with a constant supply of oxygen. Starting in the left ventricle, describe the journey blood takes in your body through the circulatory system. *(4 marks)*

Blood leaves the left ventricle and travels at high pressure to the rest of the body. It then travels into the right atrium. It then goes up to the lungs where it collects oxygen. The blood is now oxygenated. From here the heart pumps the blood back around the rest of the body.

Where possible use a flow diagram to explain a procedure / technique. Each step of the flow diagram would be worth 1 mark.

To achieve full marks you could have used part of this flow diagram (each point mentioned would be worth 1 mark, up to a maximum of 4 marks):

Left ventricle ➔ Arteries (1) ➔ Capillaries (1) ➔ Veins (1) ➔ Right atrium (1) ➔ Right ventricle (1) ➔ Lungs (1) ➔ Left atrium (1) ➔ Left ventricle

Chapter 4 — Checklist: Agriculture and farming

Tick when you:

reviewed it after your lesson	☑	☐	☐
revised once – some questions right	☑	☑	☐
revised twice – all questions right	☑	☑	☑

Move onto another topic when you have all three ticks.

Section 2 Countryside and environmental management

4.1	Photosynthesis	☐	☐	☐
4.2	What helps a plant grow big and strong?	☐	☐	☐
4.3	Intensive farming	☐	☐	☐
4.4	Organic farming	☐	☐	☐

Chapter 4 — Pre Test: Agriculture and farming

1. Write a word equation to summarise photosynthesis.

2. How do gases get into and out of a plant?

3. Where do plants obtain minerals from?

4. What do plants need magnesium for?

5. What is intensive farming?

6. Name four chemicals that can be applied to plants to help them grow.

7. How can organic farmers add minerals to the soil?

8. Name an example of biological control.

Photosynthesis

1 During photosynthesis plants turn carbon dioxide and water into sugar (glucose) and oxygen, using light energy trapped in chlorophyll.
2 Gases enter and leave the plant through stomata.
3 Water enters the plant from the soil, by osmosis into the root hair cells.

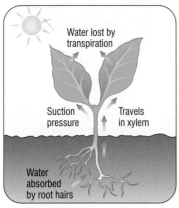

Transpiration in plants

Plants are **producers**, i.e. they make their own food by converting simple materials found in their environment into sugar. This process is called **photosynthesis**. Photosynthesis takes place inside the plant's chloroplasts, and is summarised by the equation below:

$$\text{carbon dioxide} + \text{water} \xrightarrow[\textbf{chlorophyll}]{\text{light energy trapped in}} \text{sugar} + \text{oxygen}$$
$$6\,CO_2 \qquad 6\,H_2O \qquad\qquad C_6H_{12}O_6 \qquad 6\,O_2$$

Stomata are tiny holes found on the underside of the leaf. They allow gases to diffuse into and out of the leaf:

- Carbon dioxide diffuses *in* to the plant.
- Oxygen and water vapour diffuse *out* from the plant.

Stomata are opened and closed by guard cells. They normally open during the day and close at night.

Water moves by osmosis into the root hair cells and is then transported around the plant in **xylem** vessels. As water evaporates from the leaves, more is drawn up through the plant. This is called **transpiration**.

The faster photosynthesis occurs, the more glucose is made, so the quicker the plant grows. There are four factors that affect the rate of photosynthesis:

- Light intensity
- Concentration of carbon dioxide
- Availability of water
- Surrounding temperature.

CHECK YOURSELF

1 What is a producer?
2 What structure carries water around a plant?
3 What is the role of chlorophyll in photosynthesis?

What helps a plant grow big and strong?

1 Plants use the glucose they make during photosynthesis for energy, growth and repair.
2 For healthy growth, plants need four main minerals – nitrogen, phosphorous, potassium and magnesium.
3 If the soil they are growing in lacks minerals, farmers can add more by using fertilisers.

EXAM HINTS

Check your answers! When you have finished your exam, try to leave enough time to go back over your answers. You can often pick up lots of extra marks this way.

Some of the glucose made by photosynthesis is used in respiration to release energy. Some is stored as starch. The rest is converted into cellulose, which is needed to make plant cell walls, and proteins needed for growth and repair.

Mineral needed	Role of mineral in the plant	Symptoms of mineral deficiency
Nitrates (contain nitrogen)	For healthy growth. Nitrates are involved in making DNA and amino acids. The amino acids join together to form proteins, which are needed for cell growth	Older leaves are yellowed and growth is stunted
Phosphates (contain phosphorus)	For healthy roots	Younger leaves have a purple tinge and roots grow poorly
Potassium	For healthy leaves and flowers	Yellow leaves with dead areas on them
Magnesium	For making chlorophyll	Leaves turn pale and then yellow

CHECK YOURSELF

1 What would a plant look like that is lacking phosphorus?
2 How do plants use glucose?

4.3 Intensive farming

KEY POINTS

1 Intensive farming produces as much food as possible, by making the best use of land, plants and animals.
2 Chemicals are routinely applied to plants to assist their growth; these include fertilisers, pesticides, herbicides and fungicides.
3 Animals are kept in strictly controlled environments so they use all their energy for growth. Factors that are controlled include their diet, temperature, amount of space, and the use of antibiotics.

Intensive farming produces as much food as possible, by making the best use of land, plants and animals. This makes the food produced as cheap as possible.

In intensive farming, chemicals can be applied to both plants and animals to ensure that they grow as fast as possible. They can also stop diseases from spreading. They include:

- **Artificial fertilisers** – They give a plant the nutrients that it needs to grow effectively.
- **Pesticides** – They kill insects, which may eat the crop.
- **Herbicides** – They kill other plants (weeds), which would compete with the crop for water, nutrients and space.
- **Fungicides** – They kill fungi, which can damage the crop.

Intensively farmed animals are kept in strictly controlled environments. This makes the animals increase in size more quickly. Examples include chickens, pigs and cattle.

Factor controlled	Reason for use
Food supply	High protein diet for rapid increase in body mass
Temperature	Environment kept warm. Animals waste less energy heating their own bodies
Space	Restricted movement. Animals do not waste energy moving around
Antibiotics	These are given to animals to prevent the spread of disease
Safety of enclosure	Animals are kept safe from predators

Intensively farmed chickens

CHECK YOURSELF

1 What is the difference between a pesticide and a herbicide?

2 Why do intensive farmers keep animals in strictly controlled environments?

3 Why do intensive farmers give healthy animals antibiotics?

4.4 Organic farming

KEY POINTS

1 Organic farming uses natural methods of producing crops and rearing animals.
2 Artificial chemicals are not used and animals roam freely.
3 Instead of using fertilisers, farmers use manure and compost, rotate crops and plant leguminous plants to add nutrients to the soil.
4 Biological control techniques are used to kill pests, and weeds are removed by hand or machines.

BUMP UP YOUR GRADE

If asked to compare the two types of farming, stick to the facts. Answers such as 'intensive farming is cruel' will not gain credit. To gain a mark you could say 'some people think intensive farming is cruel, as animals are often kept in very small spaces'.

CHECK YOURSELF

1 How do organic farmers avoid the use of pesticides?
2 Describe the conditions under which organic animals are kept.

Organic farming uses natural methods of producing crops and rearing animals. Artificial chemicals are not used and animals roam as freely as possible. Many people believe organic food is healthier and tastes better. However, organically produced food takes longer to produce than intensively farmed food, and is therefore often more expensive.

Crops can be grown effectively without using chemicals by:

- Adding nutrients to the soil by adding manure or compost.
- Rotating crops, because different crops take different nutrients from the soil.
- Planting leguminous plants like clover, because they add nitrates to the soil.

Farmers exploit natural predator-prey relationships to kill pests: this is called **biological control**. Predators (normally insects) are grown in large numbers, and then released onto crops where they eat the pests. For example, ladybirds can be used to eat aphids. Sometimes moulds and fungi are used to kill pests by infecting the pest with a disease. **Selective breeding** techniques are also used to produce new varieties of crops that are more resistant to pests and disease.

Farmers sometimes remove weeds by hand, however this is time-consuming, and not practical on a large scale. Machines have been developed to help weed large crop areas without damaging the crop. This method works well on crops that are grown in rows, such as vegetables.

How are animals reared organically?

Diet
Organic food is fed to the animals.

Space
Animals are allowed to roam as freely as possible.

Drugs
Animals are not given artificial growth hormones. Antibiotics are not used unless an animal is ill.

Security
Animals are usually kept indoors at night for safety from predators.

Chapter 4 — End of chapter questions

1 How does water move into root hair cells from the soil?
2 Name the four factors that affect the rate of photosynthesis.
3 What do plants need nitrates for?
4 How can farmers add extra minerals to the soil?
5 What is a 'fungicide'?
6 Why do intensive farmers restrict an animal's movement?
7 What is organic farming?
8 What techniques do organic farmers employ instead of using herbicides?

Chapter 5 — Checklist: Useful organisms

Tick when you:

reviewed it after your lesson	☑	☐	☐
revised once – some questions right	☑	☑	☐
revised twice – all questions right	☑	☑	☑

Move onto another topic when you have all three ticks.

Section 2 Countryside and environmental management

5.1 What products can we make using organisms? ☐ ☐ ☐

5.2 Making bread, beer and wine ☐ ☐ ☐

5.3 Using microorganisms to make cheese and yoghurt ☐ ☐ ☐

5.4 Selective breeding ☐ ☐ ☐

5.5 What is genetic engineering? ☐ ☐ ☐

Chapter 5 — Pre Test: Useful organisms

1. What is the origin of the leather used to make a leather jacket?

2. Where are many of our medical drugs derived from?

3. What happens during fermentation?

4. Which microorganism is used in the manufacture of bread, beer and wine?

5. How do bacteria make lactic acid?

6. What are the two useful characteristics of lactic acid in making yoghurt?

7. How do farmers selectively breed cows?

8. What characteristic would a farmer look for when breeding hens?

9. What is genetic engineering?

10. Name an example of one genetically modified plant and one animal.

5.1 What products can we make using organisms?

- **Food** – Many products are made from plants and animals, as well as food. Yeast and bacteria are also involved in making food and drink products like beer and cheese.
- **Fabrics** – Many fabrics are made from both animal materials (like wool, silk and leather) and plants (like cotton and linen). Originally all fabric dyes had a plant or animal origin.
- **Medicines** – Plant extracts from the rainforests form the basis of nearly half of the medicines used today. These include anaesthetics, contraceptives and cancer drugs. Microorganisms also play a large role in the pharmaceutical industry. A fungus is used to make penicillin and bacteria are involved in making insulin.

EXAM HINTS

Numerical questions require you to use units. There is often a mark available for writing the correct unit on an answer.

CHECK YOURSELF

1 Name three products that have a plant origin.

2 Name three products that have an animal origin.

3 Name three products that microorganisms are involved in producing.

5.2 Making bread, beer and wine

Yeast is a fungus, which is needed to make bread, beer and wine. These three products are made using a chemical reaction called **fermentation**. Fermentation is an example of **anaerobic respiration** – the yeast respires without oxygen to ferment sugar, producing alcohol and carbon dioxide. Fermentation can be summarised in the chemical equation:

glucose $\rightarrow$ ethanol (alcohol) + carbon dioxide
$C_6H_{12}O_6$ $2C_2H_5OH$ $2CO_2$

Enzymes found in yeast can be used to speed up the process of fermentation. The ideal conditions for fermentation are:

- a good supply of glucose
- no oxygen present
- a temperature between 15°C and 25°C.

To make bread, flour, water, sugar and yeast are mixed to make dough. The yeast ferments the sugar into ethanol and carbon dioxide, making the dough rise. When the dough is baked the ethanol evaporates.

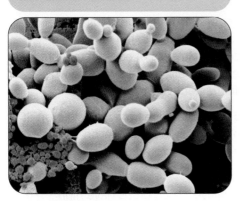

Microscopic image of yeast

BUMP UP YOUR GRADE

At foundation level, you will be expected to know the fermentation word equation. To get a grade B or better, you will be expected to know and be able to use the balanced symbol equation.

CHECK YOURSELF

1 What happens to the alcohol produced when yeast ferments sugar in bread production?

2 What are the optimum conditions for yeast to work in?

5.3 Using microorganisms to make cheese and yoghurt

KEY POINTS

1 Bacteria are used to ferment lactose into lactic acid in the production of cheese and yoghurt.
2 Both products are made from milk, but as well as adding bacteria to milk, rennet also has to be added to make cheese.

GET IT RIGHT!

Both cheese and yoghurt are produced from milk. You need to learn the similarities and differences between the added ingredients used in the two production methods, and explain why these lead to different products.

In both cheese and yoghurt production, bacteria are used to ferment lactose (milk sugar) into lactic acid.

To make cheese:

● Bacteria and rennet are added to milk. Rennet contains the enzyme rennin, which changes milk protein into casein (curd). This makes the milk curdle and separate into curds and whey.
● Whey (mainly water) is drained off and the curds are pressed to make the cheese solid.
● The cheese is left to ripen to improve its flavour and consistency.

To make yoghurt:

● Milk is boiled, then allowed to cool and bacteria are added.
● The milk is kept warm for several hours allowing the bacteria to multiply and ferment lactose.
● The lactic acid produced curdles the milk into yoghurt. It also restrains the growth of harmful bacteria, increasing the time that yoghurt can be kept and eaten safely.

CHECK YOURSELF

1 What two substances are added to milk to make yoghurt?

2 What does whey mainly consist of?

5.4 Selective breeding

KEY POINTS

1 To produce plants and animals that display desired characteristics, farmers choose which plants or animals should mate: **selective breeding**.
2 However this process takes several generations and is not very accurate. It also reduces the gene pool.

CHECK YOURSELF

1 What characteristics would a farmer be looking for in a sheep?

2 Name two advantages of selectively breeding crops.

Farmers often select the animals they keep, or plants they grow, by their characteristics. These characteristics are advantageous to the farmer, e.g. sheep that produce lots of wool or chickens that lay lots of eggs. To ensure that they maintain their stock of desired plants or animals, farmers choose which plants or animals should mate. This is called **selective breeding**.

Selective breeding of wheat has changed its appearance from the wild crop. It has large ears with many seeds that ripen at the same time, now on strong stalks that grow to the same height. This makes the crop much easier to harvest.

As well as producing high yields, many selectively bred crops have high resistance to disease. However, selective breeding reduces variation by reducing the number of genes (the **gene pool**) from which a species is created. This means that if a new disease arises, an organism may not exist that contains the gene for resistance to this disease. This could result in a species becoming extinct.

KEY POINTS

1 Foreign genes can be inserted into an organism so that the organism displays desired characteristics.
2 This is called **genetic engineering**.
3 It occurs in one generation and is more accurate than selective breeding.

BUMP UP YOUR GRADE

Make sure you know what the key words mean. These are highlighted in **bold** in this revision guide.

CHECK YOURSELF

1 Name two advantages of genetic engineering over selective breeding.

2 What are foreign genes?

Selective breeding does produce animals with desired characteristics, but it is a slow and inaccurate process. Scientists are now able to alter an organism's genes to produce desired characteristics. This is called **genetic engineering** (or **genetic modification**) and can happen in one generation. Examples include:

- Genetically modified cotton, which has a high cotton yield and pest resistance.
- The genetic engineering of the bacteria *E.Coli* to produce insulin.

To genetically engineer an organism, genes from another organism (foreign genes) are inserted into plant or animal cells at a very early stage in their development. As the organism develops it will display the characteristics of the foreign genes.

Animals are genetically modified in a similar way, by inserting the required genes into an embryo. This technique is used to modify sheep to produce pharmaceuticals in their milk.

A useful gene is removed from the nucleus of a donor cell.

The foreign gene is then put into a circular piece of DNA called a **plasmid**. This is now known as a piece of **recombinant DNA**.

The recombinant DNA is put into a bacterial cell.

The bacteria reproduce lots of times, producing lots of copies of the recombinant DNA.

Plant cells are infected with the bacteria. The foreign gene becomes integrated with the DNA of the plant cells.

The plants cells are placed in a growing medium to grow into plants. These plants will have the desired characteristics.

Chapter 5 — End of chapter questions

1 Name a plant that can be used to dye fabrics.

2 Does silk have a plant or animal origin?

3 Write the word equation for fermentation.

4 What is the proper name for milk sugar?

5 Name a disadvantage of selectively breeding plants and animals.

6 At what stage in an animal's development must foreign genes be inserted to create a genetically engineered organism?

Chapter 6 — Checklist: Managing the environment

Tick when you:

reviewed it after your lesson	☑	☐	☐
revised once – some questions right	☑	☑	☐
revised twice – all questions right	☑	☑	☑

Move onto another topic when you have all three ticks.

Section 2 Countryside and environmental management

6.1	Elements, compounds and mixtures	☐	☐	☐
6.2	Materials we take from the environment	☐	☐	☐
6.3	Chemical shorthand	☐	☐	☐
6.4	Getting useful metals from the Earth	☐	☐	☐
6.5	Advantages and disadvantages of using natural resources	☐	☐	☐

Chapter 6 — Pre Test: Managing the environment

1. Describe the differences between elements, mixtures and compounds.

2. Is H_2O an element or a compound?

3. Name three substances we can use straight from the ground.

4. Which substance is fractional distillation used to separate?

5. Which elements are present in CH_3COOH?

6. How many hydrogen atoms are there in two molecules of H_2O?

7. What is an 'ore'?

8. What is a 'reducing agent'?

9. What are the benefits to the local area if a mine is opened?

10. What are the environmental costs of mining?

6.1 Elements, compounds and mixtures

AQA EXAMINER SAYS...

Learning the symbols of the most common elements will speed up your ability to identify them. Make sure you learn those listed in Appendix D of the specification.

All substances you meet can be divided up into elements, compounds and mixtures. You need to be able to tell which is which. (It's really quite easy!)

- **Elements** – These are substances where all the atoms are the same. If you can see its name on the **periodic table**, then you can be sure it's an element. The diagram is of atoms in a metallic element, like gold. If we use symbols instead of the picture, we'd just write 'Au'.

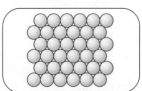

All the elements are listed in the periodic table (below).

- **Compounds** – These are substances where different elements are **bonded** (chemically attached) to each other. This is easy to see if you're given a diagram like this (it's water, by the way). If symbols are used, you'll be able to see the symbol for more than one element – for water this would be H_2O.

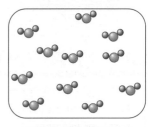

- **Mixtures** – These are combinations of different elements or compounds. They haven't been chemically joined together. Look at the diagram: there are two different types of atom 'hiding' between the water molecules.

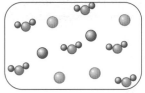

1	2												3	4	5	6	7	0
																		4 **He** helium 2
7 **Li** lithium 3	9 **Be** beryllium 4												11 **B** boron 5	12 **C** carbon 6	14 **N** nitrogen 7	16 **O** oxygen 8	19 **F** fluorine 9	20 **Ne** neon 10
23 **Na** sodium 11	24 **Mg** magnesium 12												27 **Al** aluminium 13	28 **Sl** silicon 14	31 **P** phosphorus 15	32 **S** sodium 16	35.5 **Cl** chlorine 17	40 **Ar** argon 18
39 **K** potassium 19	40 **Ca** calcium 20	45 **Sc** scandium 21	48 **Ti** thallium 22	51 **V** vanadium 23	52 **Cr** chromium 24	55 **Mn** manganese 25	56 **Fe** iron 26	59 **Co** cobalt 27	59 **Ni** nickel 28	63.5 **Cu** copper 29	65 **Zn** zinc 30	70 **Ga** gallium 31	73 **Ge** germanium 32	75 **As** arsenic 33	79 **Se** selenium 34	80 **Br** bromine 35	84 **Kr** krypton 36
85 **Rb** rubidium 37	88 **Sr** strontium 38	89 **Y** yttrium 39	91 **Zr** zirconium 40	93 **Nb** niobium 41	96 **Mo** molybdenum 42	[98] **Tc** technetium 43	101 **Ru** ruthenium 44	103 **Rh** rhodium 45	106 **Pd** palladium 46	108 **Ag** silver 47	112 **Cd** cadmium 48	115 **In** indium 49	119 **Sn** tin 50	122 **Sb** antimony 51	128 **Te** tellurium 52	127 **I** iodine 53	131 **Xe** zenon 54
133 **Cs** cesium 55	137 **Ba** barium 56	139 **La*** lanthanum 57	178 **Hf** hafnium 72	181 **Ta** tantalum 73	184 **W** tungsten 74	186 **Re** rhenium 75	190 **Os** osmium 76	192 **Ir** iridium 77	195 **Pt** platinum 78	197 **Au** gold 79	201 **Hg** mercury 80	204 **Tl** thallium 81	207 **Pb** lead 82	209 **Bi** bismuth 83	[209] **Po** polonium 84	[210] **At** astatine 85	[222] **Rn** radon 86
[223] **Fr** francium 87	[226] **Ra** radium 88	[227] **Ac*** actinium 88	[261] **Rf** rutherfordium 104	[262] **Db** dubnium 105	[266] **Sg** seaborgium 106	[264] **Bh** bohrium 107	[277] **Hs** hassium 108	[268] **Mt** meitnerium 109	[271] **Ds** darmstadium 110	[272] **Rg** roentgenium 111							

Key

relative atomic mass
atomic symbol
name
atomic (proton) number

1
H
hydrogen
1

Elements with atomic numbers 112–116 have been reported but not fully authenticated

* The Lanthanides (atomic numbers 58–71) and the Actinides (atomic numbers 90–103) have been omitted.

Cu and **Cl** have not been rounded to the nearest whole number.

Periodic Table

GET IT RIGHT!

Don't mistake a mixture for a compound just because it contains one! Check how many different substances there are.

CHECK YOURSELF

1 Is sugar an element or a compound?

2 Which of the three pictures above could be salty water?

3 What is the difference between a compound and a mixture?

6.2 Materials we take from the environment

1 Gold, limestone, marble and sulfur can be used straight from the ground.
2 Rock salt needs to be separated by filtration.
3 Crude oil needs to be separated by fractional distillation.

GET IT RIGHT!

Most salt comes from rock salt, which is mined from the ground – **not** from the sea!

We rely on materials we take from the environment for many things:

- Some of these materials can be used straight away when we find them.
- Some materials need to be separated first, so we can get at the useful stuff.

Materials we can use straight away are things like:

- Gold (used for jewellery and electronics).
- Limestone and marble (used for buildings and statues).
- Sulfur (used for making other chemicals like sulfuric acid).

Materials we have to separate first are things like:

- Rock salt (we have to get rid of the rock so we can use the salt).
- Crude oil (this contains many chemicals we can put to different uses).

Rock salt is a mixture of rock and salt that can be dug out of the ground. Because the salt is soluble, we can dissolve it and then filter out the rock.

Crude oil is used for lots of things, including: fuels, plastics, paints, medicines and road surfaces. It's made of chemicals called **hydrocarbons**. Hydrocarbons can be separated because they boil at different temperatures. This is done by **fractional distillation**.

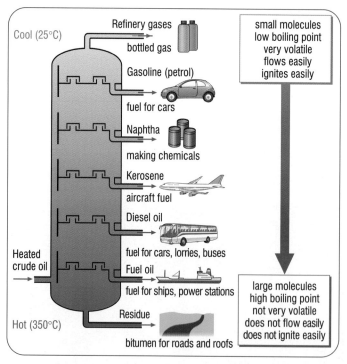

Fractional distillation in industry

1 Why is sulfur a useful material?

2 What needs to be separated from salt that is dug from the ground?

3 What is the difference between the chemicals in crude oil that lets us separate them?

6.3 Chemical shorthand

We often use **symbols** when writing about chemicals. This saves time – and ink!

You need to learn the most common symbols from the periodic table. They are:

Non-metals		Metals	
Element	Chemical symbol	Element	Chemical symbol
Argon	Ar	Aluminium	Al
Bromine	Br	Sodium	Na
Carbon	C	Calcium	Ca
Chlorine	Cl	Gold	Au
Hydrogen	H	Iron	Fe
Nitrogen	N	Lead	Pb
Oxygen	O	Magnesium	Mg
Phosphorus	P	Potassium	K
Silicon	Si	Silver	Ag
Sulfur	S	Zinc	Zn

GET IT RIGHT!

Some symbols are easily confused – don't mix up sodium and sulfur, or chlorine and carbon!

Cover up the symbols and see how many you can remember. Get a friend to help you by calling out random elements for you to give the symbols for. You also need to learn the formulas for some common molecules. They are listed in the tables.

When different elements are combined in compounds, numbers are used too. Don't let them confuse you! A small number after a symbol tells you how many atoms of that element there are. A big number before a symbol tells you how many whole molecules there are. $3H_2O$ means *three* lots of H_2O, which contains *two* hydrogen atoms for each oxygen atom.

Here are the formulas of some elements that exist as molecules:

Element	Formula of molecule
Chlorine	Cl_2
Hydrogen	H_2
Nitrogen	N_2
Oxygen	O_2

Compound	Formula
Ammonia	NH_3
Carbon dioxide	CO_2
Ethanol	C_2H_5OH
Hydrogen chloride	HCl
Methane	CH_4
Water	H_2O

CHECK YOURSELF

1 What are the chemical symbols for magnesium, chlorine and lead?

2 How many hydrogen atoms are there in a molecule of ethanol (C_2H_5OH)?

3 What is the formula for methane?

6.4 Getting useful metals from the Earth

KEY POINTS

1 An ore is rock with a high metal content (often containing metal oxides).
2 Reducing agents remove oxygen from ores.
3 Carbon and carbon monoxide are reducing agents.

GET IT RIGHT!

Learning all these reactions might look difficult at first. Just learn the word equations first, then match up the names of the chemicals to their symbols.

Metals are hugely important to society. Millions of tons of metal **ores** are mined and processed every year.

Most ores are metals combined with oxygen. To get rid of the oxygen:

- We need to **reduce** the ore.
- Chemicals that do this are called **reducing agents**.
- They have to be more reactive than the metal being reduced.

Extracting iron in a blast furnace:

- The reducing agent is carbon monoxide.
- The carbon monoxide is formed by burning lots of coke (a form of coal).

$$\text{C} + \text{O}_2 \rightarrow \text{CO}_2$$
carbon   oxygen   carbon dioxide

Then the carbon dioxide reacts with more coke to produce carbon monoxide:

$$\text{C} + \text{CO}_2 \rightarrow 2\text{CO}$$
carbon   carbon dioxide   carbon monoxide

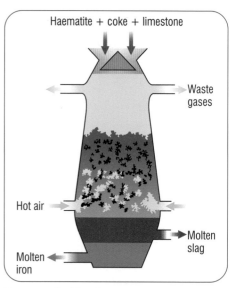

Haematite + coke + limestone

Waste gases

Hot air

Molten slag

Molten iron

Diagram of a blast furnace

The carbon monoxide then reduces the iron oxide:

$$3\text{CO} + \text{Fe}_2\text{O}_3 \rightarrow 3\text{CO}_2 + 2\text{Fe}$$
carbon monoxide   iron oxide   carbon dioxide   iron

Limestone is added to the blast furnace. This forms a substance called **slag**.

Extracting lead from lead oxide:

- Lead is extracted in a similar way to iron, but a blast furnace isn't needed.
- This is what happens:

lead oxide   carbon   →   lead   carbon monoxide
$$\text{PbO} + \text{C} \rightarrow \text{Pb} + \text{CO}$$

- Some of the carbon monoxide also reacts with the lead oxide, reducing it even more.

CHECK YOURSELF

1 Which element are metals often combined with in ores?

2 What are the three chemical reactions that happen in a blast furnace?

3 Name the reducing agents used to extract iron and lead.

6.5 Advantages and disadvantages of using natural resources

students' book
page 132

KEY POINTS

1 Extracting natural materials benefits society but at the cost of the environment.
2 Natural resources should be managed sustainably to reduce environmental damage.

CHECK YOURSELF

1 Write down as many benefits of mining as you can. Can you think of any that aren't listed on this page?

2 Describe how a mine can damage (a) the local environment, and (b) the global environment.

3 What do the terms 'sustainability' and 'stakeholder' mean?

EXAM HINTS

Check the wording of a question on this topic. Is it asking you to *list* (just write down bullet points), or *describe* (explain what each point means) the costs and benefits of mining?

As a society, we take a lot of materials from the environment. You need to be able to weigh up the costs and benefits of this kind of activity:

Benefits	Costs
• We need the materials to make: buildings, cars, electronics, plastics, paints, medicines, *virtually everything* • We can sell the materials to make money • Hundreds of thousands of people have jobs mining and processing natural resources	• Mines and quarries spoil the landscape • Mine closures cause loss of jobs • Processing ores releases carbon dioxide into the atmosphere, adding to global warming • Poisonous chemicals can be washed out of mines into rivers and lakes

Look at the lists above and decide which costs and benefits affect society, and which affect the environment.

Of course, the need for these materials is too great for us to stop mining. We need to manage the environment responsibly.

Sustainable development
Sustainability is using these resources in a way that balances human and environmental needs:

• The environmental impact of mines needs to be carefully monitored.
• Environmental damage needs to be minimised.

Involving stakeholders
Stakeholders are the people affected by an activity.

Individuals and communities whose lifestyles may change because of mining operations should be consulted before a mine or quarry is opened.

Chapter 6 End of chapter questions

1 Use diagrams to explain how oxygen is an element but carbon dioxide is a compound.

2 Describe the usefulness of crude oil, and how we separate the different hydrocarbons in it.

3 What is the chemical formula for ammonia?

4 Draw a sketch of a blast furnace, showing which raw materials go in and which products come out.

5 Describe the concerns a member of the public might have about a mine opening in their area.

Tick when you:

reviewed it after your lesson	☑	☐	☐
revised once – some questions right	☑	☑	☐
revised twice – all questions right	☑	☑	☑

Move onto another topic when you have all three ticks.

Section 2 Countryside and environmental management

7.1 Finding fossil fuels ☐ ☐ ☐

7.2 Tour of a power station ☐ ☐ ☐

7.3 Problems with fossil fuels ☐ ☐ ☐

7.4 The nuclear alternative ☐ ☐ ☐

7.5 Renewable energy resources ☐ ☐ ☐

Chapter 7 — Pre Test: Energy sources

1. **Explain why coal is a non-renewable source of energy.**

2. **Draw a simple block diagram showing how electricity is made in a power station.**

3. **What else is oil used for, apart from as a fuel?**

4. **Is nuclear power a renewable alternative to fossil fuels? Explain your answer.**

5. **Name three renewable alternative energy resources.**

---

students' book page 138

7.1 Finding fossil fuels

KEY POINTS

1. Fuels are chemicals that release energy when you burn them.
2. Coal, crude oil and natural gas are fossil fuels.
3. Because fossil fuels take so long to form, they are non-renewable.

Coal burns with an orange-yellow flame

In the UK, we use large amounts of **coal** and **natural gas** to generate electricity, as well as using many products of **crude oil** to provide fuel for vehicles.

Fuels release stored **chemical energy** when they are burned – this is called **combustion**. Coal, crude oil and natural gas are called **fossil fuels** because they are the remains of organisms (plants or animals) that lived millions of years ago.

Coal was made from the remains of plants that grew about 300 million years ago. When they died, the energy stored in them was preserved. Crude oil and natural gas were made from the remains of tiny sea creatures and plants from about 150 million years ago.

Because our fossil fuels have taken so long to form, once we run out of them we cannot make any more. For this reason, we call them **non-renewable** resources.

GET IT RIGHT!

Fossil fuels take *millions* of years to form – not just hundreds or thousands.

CHECK YOURSELF

1. Can you name two fuels that are renewable?
2. Why is it a problem that fossil fuels are non-renewable?

40

7.2 Tour of a power station

A power station

AQA EXAMINER SAYS…

The heart of any power station is the generator (or dynamo) – the electromagnetic device that turns kinetic energy into electricity.

This is how electricity is made in power stations:

A **fuel** is burned, releasing heat.

↓

This heat is used to boil water, creating very hot **steam**.

↓

The steam is forced into **turbines** – huge blades that are made to spin.

↓

The turbines are connected to a **generator** (dynamo) – when this spins it makes electricity.

Chemical energy
↓
Heat energy
↓
Kinetic energy
↓
Electrical energy

At each stage, some energy is wasted – especially in the left-over steam that leaves the cooling towers at the end. Engineers are working to make power stations more efficient so that our remaining **fossil fuels** last longer.

EXAM HINTS

Most energy resource questions involve talking about energy transfers. This means that you need to know what the nine types of energy are – and talk about transfers in terms of 'from' and 'to'.

CHECK YOURSELF

1 Describe the journey of the huge amounts of water that pass through a power station.
2 An average power station can produce 100 million watts (100 megawatts) of power. How many 100W light bulbs could this light?

7.3 Problems with fossil fuels

Coal reserves should last into the twenty-third century, **oil** and **gas** might run out by 2050! Fossil fuels are **non-renewable** – once they're gone, they're gone.

Crude oil also provides us with a wide range of products, including plastics, paints and some medicines. Not only does this mean we're using up the oil faster all the time, but that we'll face even more problems when it runs out. The other big issue with the use of fossil fuels is pollution:

- **Combustion** produces **carbon dioxide**, which is a **greenhouse gas** that contributes to **global warming** by trapping heat from the Sun.
- **Soot, carbon monoxide** and **nitrogen oxides** (NO_x) are also produced – these can all cause health problems.
- The NO_x and **sulfur dioxide** produced also create **acid rain**, which is harmful to plants, animals and buildings.

GET IT RIGHT!

Remember that 'renewable' means that it can be replaced. Don't get this confused with 'recyclable' or 'reusable', which mean different things.

CHECK YOURSELF

1 Which gases produced from the combustion of fossil fuels could damage your health?
2 Explain why plastics recycling could help our oil supplies to last a little longer.

BUMP UP YOUR GRADE

Read up a little on acid rain and the greenhouse effect to help you answer questions in more detail.

The nuclear alternative

AQA EXAMINER SAYS...

Nuclear power is sometimes grouped in with the fossil fuels because it is non-renewable, but other times it is treated as an alternative energy resource. The way to think about all of these energy resources is to consider and compare their advantages and disadvantages.

Uranium is a **nuclear fuel** – it is a **radioactive** element that releases energy (its atoms break apart in a process called **fission**). Huge amounts of heat are produced, so it can be used to heat steam in a power station.

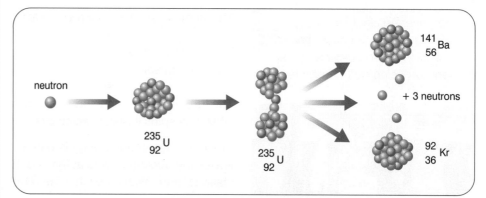

Nuclear fission of uranium

A nuclear power station

Will nuclear power take over as the fossil fuels run out? Consider the arguments for and against:

For	Against
Uranium releases 10 000 times as much energy as coal does.	Uranium is non-renewable – it has to be quarried and so will eventually run out.
It is quite cheap, nuclear power costs about the same as coal.	The waste produced is radioactive – which is expensive to dispose of.
It doesn't produce polluting gases.	There have been several nuclear power station accidents.
Only a small amount of waste is produced.	Give out radiation

Nuclear power could produce the energy we need to fill in the gap that will be left as the fossil fuels begin to run out, but it can't be a long-term solution to our energy problems.

CHECK YOURSELF

1 What arguments would you use to persuade people that greater use of nuclear power is a bad idea?

2 Why is nuclear power sometimes described as clean and at other times as producing dangerous wastes?

7.5 Renewable energy resources

CHECK YOURSELF

1 Why do we need to develop our use of alternative energy resources?

2 Which alternative energy resources could you use at home to cut down your electricity bill?

3 Explain why biomass produces more pollution than the other alternative energy resources.

More than 90% of our electricity in the UK comes from non-renewable resources. We need to develop **alternative** energy resources that are sustainable (**renewable**), clean and preferably cheap.

There are several alternative resources in development:

Energy resource	Advantages	Disadvantages
Wind power – turbine blades spin in the wind, turning a generator	Renewable, clean, cheap	Noisy / ugly, weather-dependent
HEP – water runs down from a high reservoir, turning turbines as it falls	Renewable, power on demand	Environmental impact, not many good places in UK
Solar power – Solar cells absorb the Sun's energy and turn it into electricity	Renewable, clean, cheap	Daytime / weather-dependent, small scale
Wave / Tidal power – the motion of the oceans is used to make electricity	Renewable, clean, we have tides every day	Environmental impact, few good places in UK, waves can be unreliable
Biomass – plant or animal products are burnt to release heat	Renewable, power on demand, can also be disposal of wastes	Burning fuels causes pollution

None of these resources is yet well enough developed to replace fossil fuels – but we need to keep trying!

EXAM HINTS

Look for links between the renewable energy resources, e.g. all are renewable – but most are not always available. Looking for rules and exceptions, like this, is a good way to revise.

Chapter 7   End of chapter questions

1 Describe how coal was formed.

2 Explain why power stations are not very efficient.

3 Summarise the main problems with our use of fossil fuels.

4 If you wanted to convince people to use nuclear power more, what arguments would you use?

5 The renewable energy resource most used in the UK is biofuels. Why do you think this is?

1 Inside a biomass thermal power station, waste animal and plant matter are burnt to generate electricity.

   (a) Match the parts of the power station to their function by drawing a line between a copy of the boxes.

   One line has been drawn for you.

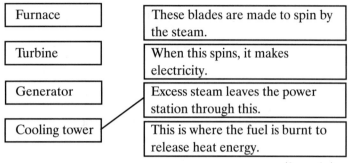

Furnace	These blades are made to spin by the steam.
Turbine	When this spins, it makes electricity.
Generator	Excess steam leaves the power station through this.
Cooling tower	This is where the fuel is burnt to release heat energy.

(3 marks)

   (b) In the sentences below, choose the correct answer in each box.

   (i) Biomass is a type of fuel that will not run out. It is called

   | recyclable   renewable   reusable | (1 mark)

   (ii) Most of our electricity comes from burning fossil fuels like | uranium   wood   coal | (1 mark)

   (iii) A clean alternative energy resource that can't be used at night is | wind   solar   tidal |(1 mark)

   (c) Complete the sentences using words from this list:

   carbon   electricity   nuclear   oil   wind

   When . . . is burned it produces gases including . . . dioxide that cause pollution. Alternative energy sources like . . . are free of pollution but unreliable.   (3 marks)

2 Coal, oil and natural gas are all from a group of similar fuels.

   (a) What do we call this group of fuels? Choose the correct answer:

   alternative   fossil   nuclear   renewable   (1 mark)

   (b) How many years do coal, oil and natural gas take to form? Choose the best answer:

   hundreds   thousands   millions   billions (1 mark)

   (c) Scientists are looking for other energy resources to replace coal, oil and natural gas when they run out.

   Fill in the gaps in this sentence with words from the list:

   geothermal   HEP   wave   wind

   The sea can provide us with . . . energy and the weather can provide us with . . . energy.   (2 marks)

(d) Give one other reason why it is a good idea to find different energy resources to use.   (1 mark)

3 Intensive farmers produce most of the developed world's food. To ensure their crops grow quickly and produce high yields they use a range of chemicals.

   (a) Match the following chemicals with their use. (4 marks)

Fertiliser	**Kills weeds**
Herbicide	**Kills fungi**
Fungicide	**Kills pests**
Pesticide	**Gives the plants the nutrients it needs to grow effectively**

   (b) Animals are kept in strictly controlled environments so that they also grow quickly. Name two factors that farmers control apart from the size of their enclosure.   (2 marks)

   (c) Why do intensive farmers restrict an animal's movement?   (1 mark)

4 Farmers choose their best animals to breed so that the offspring they produce possess desired characteristics.

   (a) What is this technique known as?   (1 mark)

   (b) Name a disadvantage to the species of the technique stated above.   (1 mark)

   Scientists are now able to alter an organism's genes by genetic engineering to have the same effect.

   (c) Name two advantages of this technique over that used by farmers.   (2 marks)

   Bacteria can be genetically engineered to produce human insulin. This is very important in the treatment of diabetes.

   (d) Describe the procedure that a scientist would follow to create bacteria that produce insulin.   (5 marks)

5 The metals we use come from ores mined from the Earth's crust. Mining ores can benefit society but can also harm the environment.

   (a) Give two advantages to society of mining, and two ways it can harm the environment.   (4 marks)

   (b) Many mines try to practise 'sustainability'. What does this mean?   (3 marks)

 Test & Assessment Interactive quizzes, answers and hints online!

The answer is worth 3 marks.

The responses worth a mark are underlined in red.

We can improve the answer in several ways:

A mark was lost because the candidate didn't *describe* the effects of the extra traffic. They should have written that the **increased traffic fumes could add to acid rain and possibly global warming**.

Mining for ores has an effect upon the environment. Environmental scientists are always employed by mining corporations to help reduce the environmental damage they do.

Describe two ways a lead mine could harm the environment.   (*4 marks*)

- A lead mine could harm the environment because of the traffic to and from the mine.
- Another way is if it rains and poisonous lead chemicals get washed into rivers - this might kill wildlife.

This just means list!

This means that you have to say how the factor increases body size.

4 marks means you will need to state and explain 4 different factors.

The answer is worth the full 4 marks.

This is a well-structured answer, because each factor is stated, and then an explanation given.

Each bullet point is worth 1 mark.

Intensive farmers raise animals in strictly controlled environments so that they increase in size as quickly as possible. State and explain the main factors controlled by intensive farmers to gain a high meat yield.   (*4 marks*)

- Food supply - animals are fed a high protein diet so that they rapidly increase their body mass.
- Temperature - animals are kept warm so they don't waste energy heating their own bodies. Therefore all energy is used for growth.
- Restricted space - animals do not waste energy moving around. Therefore all energy is used for growth.
- Antibiotics - these are given to all animals to prevent them catching a disease. Therefore they do not get ill and put on weight as quickly as possible.

Where possible organise your answers into bullet points. This focuses your answer to make sure you say enough to gain full marks, but not too much! Candidates often write too much, and lose marks by adding incorrect statements. Each wrong answer cancels out a correct answer.

If you state a factor but do not explain it, you will not receive a mark for that point.

Tick when you:

reviewed it after your lesson	☑	☐	☐
revised once – some questions right	☑	☑	☐
revised twice – all questions right	☑	☑	☑

Move onto another topic when you have all three ticks.

Section 3 The home environment

8.1	Small building blocks	☐	☐	☐
8.2	Bigger building blocks	☐	☐	☐
8.3	What's the difference between metals and non-metals?	☐	☐	☐
8.4	Covalent molecules – electron *sharing*	☐	☐	☐
8.5	Ionic compounds – electron *transfer*	☐	☐	☐
8.6	Giant covalent structures	☐	☐	☐

| Chapter 8 | Pre Test: Structure and bonding |

(1) **What is the charge on (a) an electron, (b) a proton?**

(2) **What is the difference between atoms and molecules?**

(3) **What is an 'ion'?**

(4) **Why are metals good conductors of electricity?**

(5) **Which of these is a common characteristic of non-metals? Shiny, ductile, brittle.**

(6) **What is a covalent bond?**

(7) **A compound has a boiling point of 376°C. Is it ionic or covalent?**

(8) **Salt is made of sodium ions and chloride ions. Which ion is negative and which is positive?**

(9) **Why do covalent molecules have low melting points?**

(10) **Which of these have giant molecular structures? Diamond, methane, graphite.**

8.1 Small building blocks

KEY POINTS

1 Atoms are made of positive protons, neutral neutrons and negative electrons.
2 Protons and neutrons are in the middle (nucleus) of an atom.
3 Electrons whizz around the outside.
4 The periodic table tells us how many protons there are in each type of atom. This is called the **atomic number**. It also tells you how many protons plus neutrons there are in an atom. This is called the **mass number**.

CHECK YOURSELF

1 What particles are in the nucleus of an atom?
2 What is the charge of a neutron?
3 Carbon has six protons. How many electrons does it have?

An atom is the basic building block of all chemicals, and you need to know its structure!

The middle bit of an atom is called the **nucleus**. It's made of two types of particle:

● **protons**   ● **neutrons**.

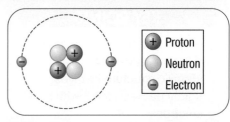

Helium atom

Whizzing around the nucleus are particles called **electrons**. These particles have different charges and masses to each other:

Particle	Where is it?	Charge	Mass
Proton	In the nucleus	+1	1
Neutron	In the nucleus	0	1
Electron	Outside the nucleus	−1	Very low

In atoms, there are always the *same* numbers of protons and electrons. This makes their charges balance out. You can find information about different atoms in the periodic table. Each different type of atom is called an **element**.

8.2 Bigger building blocks

KEY POINTS

1 Molecules are made of atoms that have been chemically bonded to each other.
2 Ions are made when atoms gain or lose electrons.
3 Gaining electrons makes a negative ion. Losing electrons makes a positive ion.

CHECK YOURSELF

1 What's the difference between an oxygen atom and an oxygen molecule?
2 If a hydrogen atom loses an electron, what charge does it now have?

Sometimes atoms are stuck together with chemical bonds, and sometimes they have lost or gained electrons. You have to recognise when this has happened.

Molecules are when two or more atoms are chemically bonded to each other. This has happened with the oxygen you're breathing right now (O_2 means there are 2 oxygen atoms in a molecule).

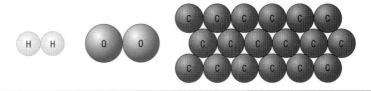

Hydrogen, oxygen and carbon atoms

If an atom loses or gains electrons, we call it an **ion**. Electrons are negatively charged. This means that gaining electrons makes a negative ion and losing electrons makes a positive ion.

BUMP UP YOUR GRADE

Remember, if a question asks you what charge an ion has, don't just say positive or negative. Count how many electrons have been lost or gained and work out *how* positive or negative it is. For example, if a copper atom has lost two electrons, it has become a +2 ion.

8.3 What's the difference between metals and non-metals?

EXAMINER SAYS...

Remember, if a question asks you to *describe* a property of metals, you need to write down what that property means. If the question says *explain*, you need to write down *why* metals have that property.

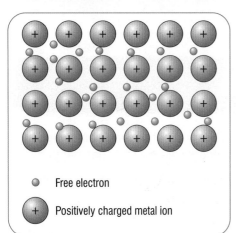

- Free electron

- Positively charged metal ion

The bonding in a metal

Metals and non-metals have different properties to each other. By looking at the properties of an element, it's usually easy to tell if it's a metal or non-metal.

1	2											3	4	5	6	7	0

Key: relative atomic mass / **atomic symbol** / name / atomic (proton) number
non-metals
metals

Simplified periodic table

* The Lanthanides (atomic numbers 58–71) and the Actinides (atomic numbers 90–103) have been omitted.

Cu and **Cl** have not been rounded to the nearest whole number.

Look at the periodic table shown here. All the metals are on the left (shown in blue) and all the non-metals are on the right (pink). As you can see, most elements are metals.

These are the usual properties of metals:

- They have high **melting** and **boiling points**.
- They are usually strong, dense and shiny.
- They can be shaped and bent.
- They conduct heat and electricity well.

Metals have most of these properties because of their structure:

- Metal structures have all the atoms (or ions) packed together really closely, making them dense and heavy.
- Some electrons are able to move freely throughout the metal. This is why metals are good at conducting heat and electricity. (See the diagram in the margin.)
- This structure also makes it easier for the atoms to slide over each other when they're pushed. This is why metals can be bent or hammered into shapes.

Non-metals have pretty much the opposite properties of metals:

- They have low melting and boiling points.
- They are less dense than metals and dull in appearance.
- They are brittle.
- They don't conduct heat and electricity well.

CHECK YOURSELF

1 Write down the chemical symbols for three metals and three non-metals.

2 Draw a diagram showing the arrangement of atoms in a metal.

3 Describe three properties of metals and three properties of non-metals.

8.4 Covalent molecules – electron *sharing*

As you know, atoms are able to make chemical bonds with each other so they 'stick together'. One type of bond is called a **covalent bond**.

When atoms bond covalently, it means they share electrons with each other. They do this to make themselves more stable. For example, hydrogen has one electron, but it 'prefers' to have two. Because of this, two hydrogen atoms can get very close and share their electrons, so they each have two.

The diagram here shows this happening:

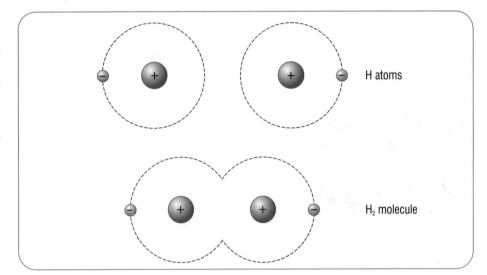

H atoms

H₂ molecule

Hydrogen atoms, and a molecule of hydrogen gas (H_2)

If a chemical only contains non-metal elements, it's covalent. Water is an example:

Weaker forces between molecules

Strong covalent bonds between atoms

Water molecules

Covalent bonds are strong, but the forces between individual molecules are quite weak. This means the molecules can be separated quite easily (they melt and boil at low temperatures).

Ionic compounds – electron *transfer*

KEY POINTS

1 Ions are formed when atoms transfer electrons.
2 These ions attract each other very strongly and this is called ionic bonding.
3 Ionic compounds have very high melting and boiling points.

As well as covalent bonding, atoms have another way of sticking together. They're able to transfer electrons between each other. This is called **ionic bonding**. Remember, if an atom loses an electron, it becomes a positive ion. If it gains an electron, it becomes a negative ion.

Positive and negative ions work pretty much the same way as north and south poles on a magnet – they *attract* each other. So, ions with opposite charges will 'stick' to each other strongly.

Ionic bonds are *very* strong. *Lots* of energy is needed to break them apart. This is why ionic compounds have such high melting and boiling points.

Usually, ionic bonds are found between metals and non-metals. They tend to make crystal structures.

One electron moves from Na to Cl

This makes Na⁺ and Cl⁻ ions

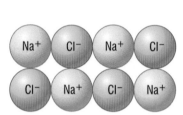

The Na⁺ and Cl⁻ ions are very strongly attracted to each other

Na and Cl atoms and Na⁺ and Cl⁻ ions

GET IT RIGHT!

If a compound contains a metal and a non-metal, it's ionic.

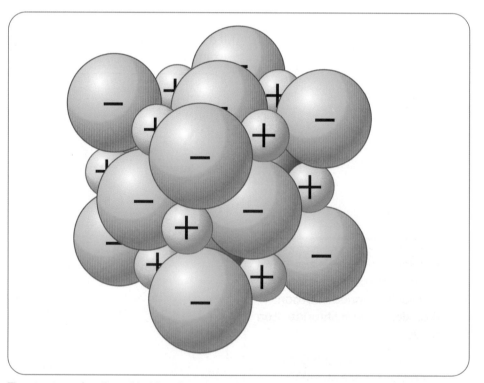

The structure of sodium chloride – the strong electrostatic forces of attraction operate in all directions

CHECK YOURSELF

1 Which of these chemicals has ionic bonding? **Sodium chloride, carbon monoxide, water**.

2 Chemical W melts at –30°C and chemical Y melts at 280°C, which one is ionic?

3 What happens to electrons in atoms when they form ions?

8.6 Giant covalent structures

KEY POINTS

1 Giant structures are made of many, many atoms.
2 Common giant structures are metals, ionic crystals, graphite and diamond.
3 Giant structures have very high melting and boiling points.

Some chemical structures are so big that a lump of it big enough to see is all one molecule.

Carbon makes some interesting giant structures you need to know about:

● **Graphite** (the 'lead' in pencils) – This is made of millions of sheets of carbon atoms arranged in hexagons. These layers are able to slide over each other, which is why graphite rubs off onto paper. The diagram only shows a small part of the billions of carbon atoms in a piece of graphite.

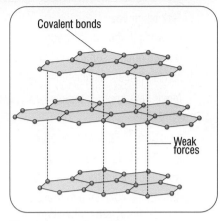

Covalent bonds

Weak forces

The structure of graphite

● **Diamond** – This is another giant carbon structure. The covalent bonds between atoms are really strong, making it one of the hardest substances in the world.

The huge number of strong bonds in giant structures gives them very high melting and boiling points.

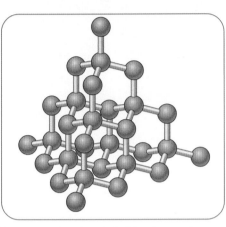

Strong covalent bonds hold a diamond together

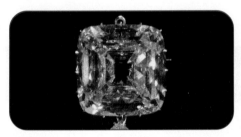

Diamond

GET IT RIGHT!

Remember the link between the structure and the melting or boiling point of a substance. Giant structures mean a high melting or boiling point.

CHECK YOURSELF

1 Diamond and sodium chloride are both giant structures. How are their bonds different?

2 Why is a lot of energy needed to melt a giant structure?

Chapter 8   End of chapter questions

1 **Name and describe the structure of the three particles in an atom.**

2 **Are metals on the left- or right-hand side of the periodic table?**

3 **Why can metals be hammered into different shapes?**

4 **The formula for methane is CH$_4$ and its boiling point is –162 °C. Explain how these two pieces of information show that methane is a covalent molecule.**

5 **What structure do ionic compounds usually have?**

6 **Name three substances with giant structures.**

Tick when you:

reviewed it after your lesson	☑	☐	☐
revised once – some questions right	☑	☑	☐
revised twice – all questions right	☑	☑	☑

Move onto another topic when you have all three ticks.

Section 3 The home environment

9.1	Materials used in construction	☐	☐	☐
9.2	The chemistry of limestone	☐	☐	☐
9.3	Using limestone to make other construction materials	☐	☐	☐
9.4	Using metals in construction	☐	☐	☐
9.5	Other materials used in construction	☐	☐	☐
9.6	Properties and uses of other construction materials	☐	☐	☐

| Chapter 9 | Pre Test: Construction materials |

1. What is the chemical name for limestone?

2. How is quicklime produced?

3. How is cement made?

4. What is the main raw material for making glass?

5. What is the difference between mortar and concrete?

6. Why are metals useful for making wires?

7. What does 'malleable' mean?

8. What is a composite material?

9. Where in the home would you find ceramics?

10. List three properties of polymers.

9.1 Materials used in construction

KEY POINTS

1 Limestone is a major construction material, and has a number of other important uses.
2 The chemical name for limestone is calcium carbonate.
3 Limestone can be converted into quicklime (calcium oxide) and slaked lime (calcium hydroxide).

Limestone is the starting point for a number of useful materials. It's also a building material in its own right.

These are the uses of limestone:

● Building material
● Making cement and mortar
● Making glass
● Treating areas affected by acid rain
● Producing iron
● Making paper.

Limestone is dug out of the ground at quarries:

A limestone quarry

Limestone is closely related to two other materials, **quicklime** and **slaked lime**. You need to know their chemical names and formulas:

CHECK YOURSELF

1 List three materials produced using limestone.
2 What are the chemical names for limestone, quicklime and slaked lime?
3 What is the chemical formula for the calcium carbonate in limestone?

Substance	Chemical name	Chemical formula
Limestone	Calcium carbonate	$CaCO_3$
Quicklime	Calcium oxide	CaO
Slaked lime	Calcium hydroxide	$Ca(OH)_2$

9.2 The chemistry of limestone

KEY POINTS

1 Limestone is converted to quicklime by heating it.
2 Quicklime is converted to slaked lime by adding water.
3 An exothermic reaction gives off heat energy.
4 An endothermic reaction absorbs heat energy.

Quicklime (calcium oxide) and slaked lime (calcium hydroxide) are both produced from limestone. They're used for making other building materials like **cement**.

To make quicklime, limestone is crushed into tiny pieces. It's then put into a lime kiln (very hot, very big) where hot air gets blown through it. When this happens, carbon dioxide is given off:

limestone → quicklime + carbon dioxide
$$CaCO_3 \rightarrow CaO + CO_2$$

Because the reaction needs heat energy to work, we call it **endothermic**.

Quicklime can be converted to slaked lime by adding water:

quicklime + water → slaked lime
$$CaO + H_2O \rightarrow Ca(OH)_2$$

This reaction releases a lot of heat energy (if you did it in your hand, you'd get a nasty burn). This type of reaction is called **exothermic**.

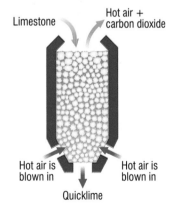

Limestone — Hot air + carbon dioxide

Hot air is blown in — Hot air is blown in

Quicklime

Diagram of a lime kiln

CHECK YOURSELF

1 What are quicklime and slaked lime used for?
2 Write the chemical equation for converting quicklime into slaked lime.
3 Why do we say limestone → quicklime is an endothermic reaction?

Using limestone to make other construction materials

1 Cement is made by roasting limestone with clay and gypsum.
2 Mortar is a mixture of cement, sand and water.
3 Concrete is a mixture of cement, sand, stones and water.
4 Glass is made by melting sand, limestone and sodium carbonate together.

GET IT RIGHT!

Make sure you can explain the differences between cement, concrete and mortar – they're easily confused!

Limestone can be used as a construction material by just stacking up big blocks of it. However, it's also used by the construction industry to make other building materials, like cement, concrete, mortar and glass.

- **Cement** is basically quicklime that's been roasted with some clay and a material called **gypsum** (calcium sulfate). Cement can be added to other materials and water. It reacts with the water to cement (glue) all the particles together.
- **Mortar** is the stuff that sticks bricks together. It's a mixture of cement, sand and water.

Working with mortar

- **Concrete** is made the same way as mortar, but also contains small stones. It's much harder than mortar – whole buildings can be made from it.

- **Glass** is also made using limestone. Glass is mainly sand with some limestone and **sodium carbonate** added. This all gets melted together, and forms glass when it cools down.

Different uses of glass

CHECK YOURSELF

1 Describe how mortar is produced from limestone.

2 What are the ingredients for making concrete?

3 As well as limestone, what is needed to make glass?

9.4 Using metals in construction

KEY POINTS

1 Metals can be used as frames or for reinforcement in construction.
2 Metals are useful in construction because of their properties

Metals are often used alongside other construction materials in building. This is because they have useful properties engineers can take advantage of.

In the exam, you need to be able to explain why a metal has been used for a particular job. Here are the words you should be using:

Working with metals

Property of metals	What it means	Why it's useful
Hard	Firm or rigid; not easily dented, crushed, or pierced	Metal parts of structures are long-lasting
Strong	Solid or robust in construction, not easily broken	Metal parts of structures don't break off easily
Malleable	Metals can be beaten into different shapes	It's fairly easy to get metal into the shape you need it
Ductile	Metals can be pulled out into fine wires	You can use metals for wiring and electrics
High melting point	Metals don't melt easily	Metal parts of structures withstand fire
Good conductors	Heat and electricity can travel through them	You can use metals to transfer energy from one place to another
High density	The atoms are packed closely together	Metal structures are solid and heavy

Turn to page 48 to remind yourself why metals have these properties.

Metals can be used for frames or for reinforcement (like in the photo). Putting iron or steel rods into concrete makes it stronger. This is because the metal makes reinforced concrete harder to crack.

This builder is making reinforced concrete

Alloys

Mixtures of metals are called alloys. They are often stronger than pure metals. We say that they have a higher **tensile strength**. Some examples of alloys are:

Name of alloy	Composition
Steel	Iron and carbon
Brass	Copper and zinc
Solder	Tin and lead

CHECK YOURSELF

Use the above table of properties to explain why:

1 Metals can be used as lightning rods (these divert lightning strikes around the outside of buildings).

2 Metals can be made into door handles.

3 Metals can be used to reinforce concrete.

9.5 Other materials used in construction

KEY POINTS

1 Ceramics are hard, strong, have high melting points and resist chemical attack.
2 Polymers are light, flexible, soft, have low melting points and are insulators.
3 Composites are combinations of existing materials, chosen to get the best properties of each.

Limestone and metals aren't the only materials used in today's buildings. Ceramics, polymers and composites are also important materials used by the construction industry.

Ceramics are materials like china, clay, brick and porcelain (most toilet bowls are made of porcelain).

They're useful because they:

- Are very hard.
- Are resistant to chemical attack.
- Have high melting points.
- Are strong (although they can crack because they're not flexible).

Polymers are materials like plastics. They're made by getting lots of tiny molecules (which we call **monomers**) to stick together into long tangled chains.

Examples of uses for polymers

The properties of polymers are:

- They have low density (they're light).
- They're flexible.
- They're soft.
- They have a low melting point.
- They insulate heat and electricity.

EXAM HINTS

Questions on this topic will often ask you to choose a material for a particular job, or explain why a particular material has been used. Make sure you know the properties of metals, ceramics, polymers and composites well, and can justify your choices.

Composites are being used more recently in construction. They're the result of putting two materials together to get the best out of both of them. For example, weaving glass fibres together and covering them in plastic makes a composite called fibreglass. It is a light but very tough material.

Fibreglass being made

CHECK YOURSELF

1 Why are ceramic tiles used on the nose-cones of space shuttles?

2 Why are polymers a good choice for cheap roofing material?

3 Describe fibreglass.

Properties and uses of other construction materials

KEY POINTS

1 Use ceramics for things you want to be strong, stand high temperatures and be wipe-clean.
2 Use polymers for things you want to be moulded into shape, light, cheap or flexible.
3 Use composites when any single material has limitations you want to get over.

Now you've got to the end of this chapter, you're a budding materials scientist! The last thing you need to know about is the kinds of uses we put these building materials to.

Ceramics are used for lots of things, including:

- Sinks
- Tiles
- Bricks
- Toilet bowls
- Space shuttle nose-cones.

Ceramics in action

Think back to the properties of ceramics – can you explain each of these uses?

Polymers are often used to replace traditional materials like wood. They've got lots of uses in construction, like:

- Windows
- Frames
- Garden furniture
- Handles
- Skirting
- Bath and shower fittings
- Electrical fittings   ...and many more.

Polymers often replace wood

Again, are you able to explain why polymers can be used for these items?

The properties of **composites** are carefully chosen by the materials that scientists use to make them. When you're explaining why a composite was used for a job, you need to know the properties of the materials in it.

For example, fibreglass is used for making boats. It's made of glass (hard) and a polymer resin (light and flexible). This makes it hard, light and flexible – ideal for boats.

CHECK YOURSELF

1 Look around the room now. Choose five items made from different materials. Try to explain why each material was chosen.

2 Reinforced glass is glass with metal wires in. How do the metal wires make the glass stronger?

3 List all the materials you could use to make a tabletop out of. What are the strengths and weaknesses of each material?

AQA EXAMINER SAYS...

You will be tested on how well you can explain choices of materials. If a question asks about a material you haven't heard of before, don't worry! As long as you know whether it's a metal, ceramic, polymer or composite, you will already know most of its properties.

Chapter 9   End of chapter questions

1 **Name two materials that are made from limestone and used in buildings.**

2 **When quicklime is changed into slaked lime, is the process exothermic or endothermic?**

3 **Which building material is made from cement, sand, small stones and water?**

4 **Which property of metals means they can be hammered into different shapes?**

5 **Which have higher melting points: ceramics or polymers?**

6 **Why is plastic a good alternative to wood for making garden furniture?**

Chapter 10 — Checklist: Using energy

Tick when you:

reviewed it after your lesson	☑	☐	☐
revised once – some questions right	☑	☑	☐
revised twice – all questions right	☑	☑	☑

Move onto another topic when you have all three ticks.

Section 3 The home environment

10.1 Energy sources in the home	☐	☐	☐
10.2 Electrical power	☐	☐	☐
10.3 Choosing and using fuses	☐	☐	☐
10.4 The cost of using electricity	☐	☐	☐
10.5 How heat is lost at home	☐	☐	☐
10.6 Evaluating efficiency	☐	☐	☐
10.7 Improving energy efficiency	☐	☐	☐

Chapter 10 — Pre Test: Using energy

1. List all of the energy sources that you use in your home – and name one use for each source.

2. If a kettle is rated as 6 A at 230 V, what is its power?

3. Describe how a fuse in a plug works.

4. If a 2 kW heater is switched on for 4 hours, how many units of electricity does it use?

5. Name and describe the three different ways that heat can move.

6. Write down the formula used to work out the efficiency of a device.

7. Why is it important for engineers to improve the efficiency of the devices they design?

10.1 Energy sources in the home

KEY POINTS

1 There are several different sources of energy that could be used in your home, including:
   - Mains electricity
   - Batteries
   - Natural Gas
   - Oil
   - Coal

2 Each of these sources has advantages and disadvantages and is best suited for particular tasks.

EXAM HINTS

When you make comparisons, say something about each energy source. Try to give an advantage and a disadvantage about each one.

This topic is all about *comparing* and *evaluating* different sources of energy. When we decide how we are going to power a particular device, there are several factors that we consider, including:

- **Availability** – Some places don't have a mains gas or electricity supply.
- **Cost** – Batteries are relatively expensive, so you wouldn't use them to power a lawnmower.
- **Portability** – Think about all the devices you wouldn't want to plug in!
- **Safety** – We don't use gas for lighting very often, as electricity is much safer.
- **Environmental impact** – Using rechargeable batteries saves money and also means that fewer dead batteries go in the bin.

CHECK YOURSELF

1 Name three different energy sources that could be used to generate the heat in a home cooker.

2 Natural gas used to be used to provide light for our homes. Why do you think it has been replaced by electricity?

3 Why do you think some houses and farms in rural areas use fuel oil to provide energy for their heating?

10.2 Electrical power

KEY POINTS

1 Electrical devices turn **electrical energy** (in **joules**) into another type of energy.

2 **Power** (in **watts**) is a measure of how fast a device uses energy.

3 The power of a device can be read from its label or calculated using the equation:

power (W) = voltage (V) × current (A)

When you switch a device on, you are giving it a supply of electrical energy, which it turns into different types. For example, a kettle turns electrical energy into heat and a bulb turns it into light.

The **rate** at which the device uses up electrical energy is called its **power**. So if a kettle uses 2000 J (or 2 kJ) of electrical energy every second, it has a power of 2000 W (or 2 kW).

Most electrical devices have an information label on them, including their power and voltage.

There is an equation that links power with voltage and current. (You need to be able to use, and rearrange it.)

Microwave Oven	
2450 MHz 230V ~ 50Hz	
Input Power	1200W
Energy Output	800W

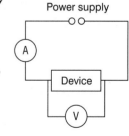

Measuring voltage and current

power (watts) = voltage (volts) × current (amperes)

EXAM HINTS

Most questions on mains electricity have a voltage of 230 V; that's what we plug into every day.

BUMP UP YOUR GRADE

Get familiar with the equation power = voltage × current, practise rearranging it to work out voltage or current.

CHECK YOURSELF

1 How much energy will a 1200 W kettle transfer in 3 minutes? (Also see p. 61.)

2 If a 60 W bulb is connected to the 230 V mains, how much current will flow through it?

3 What are the units for energy, power, voltage and current?

10.3 Choosing and using fuses

1 Fuses and circuit breakers are devices designed to break a circuit when too much electrical current is flowing.

2 You need to be able to use the equation:

$$\text{current (A)} = \frac{\text{power (W)}}{\text{voltage (V)}}$$

3 Use the current size to decide which size of fuse is needed in a circuit.

GET IT RIGHT!

Remember the rule for choosing fuses: 'slightly bigger than you need, but not too big'.

Sometimes when electrical devices go wrong, this can cause too much **current** to flow, which could:

● Make the wiring **hot** and cause a fire.
● Give you an **electrical shock**.

So we use two main types of device to safeguard against this type of problem:

● **Fuses** – They have thin pieces of wire running through them that are designed to melt if too much current flows, breaking the circuit.
● **Circuit breakers** – These detect when too much current flows and use a little electromagnet to switch the circuit off. You can sort out the problem and then switch the circuit back on.

Different types of fuse: a standard plug fuse and some car fuses

To work out what size fuse you need, you have to know how much current should flow in the circuit. If this isn't printed on the device, you can work it out using this formula:

$$\text{current (A)} = \frac{\text{power (W)}}{\text{voltage (V)}}$$

A fuse / circuit breaker box

Then pick a fuse that is *at least* that big – but not much bigger – you want it to blow before *too much* extra current flows.

BUMP UP YOUR GRADE

Practise calculating the current so that you can work out the fuse size. At home you can get the information off the back of almost any electrical device.

CHECK YOURSELF

1 Describe how a circuit breaker works.

2 A 3A fuse is designed to blow before the current flowing through it reaches 6A. What is the most powerful device that can connect through this fuse to the 230V mains electrical supply?

3 When people can't find a replacement fuse, they sometimes put a piece of kitchen foil in its place: (a) Will this work? (b) Why is doing this very dangerous?

students' book
page 192

KEY POINTS

1 Electrical devices cost most to use if they are very powerful or switched on for a long time.
2 Electrical energy is charged for in units called **kilowatt hours**.
3 The amount of energy used can be worked out using the formula:

energy (J) = power (W) × time (s)

Electrical devices can cost a lot of money to use if they need a lot of energy, which means either they are:

- Very **powerful** – so they are using a lot of energy every second, or
- used a lot – the amount of energy they use adds up over **time**.

There is a formula for working out the amount of energy that a device uses:

$$\text{energy (joules)} = \text{power (watts)} \times \text{time (s)}$$

The electricity companies charge us for the amount of energy we use – but the **joule** is a small amount of energy – a better sized one is given by:

- Using **kilowatts** instead of **watts** as their power unit.
- Using **hours** instead of **seconds** for their time units.

This gives them a larger unit for energy, the **kilowatt hour**, and the equation becomes:

$$\text{energy (kWh)} = \text{power (kW)} \times \text{time (h)}$$

A kWh is the energy used by a 100 W bulb in 10 hours (instead of a tenth of a second) and is usually priced at about 8p (written: 8 p/kWh).

Electrical meters measure how much electrical energy your house uses. The dials on your meter tell the companies how many units (kWh) of electricity you have used, so they know how much to charge you.

Wheel-style electricity meter

Dial-style electricity meter

GET IT RIGHT!

Always check the units you are using in electrical cost questions: power in kilowatts and time in hours. Practise converting numbers like 1200 W or 30 minutes.

BUMP UP YOUR GRADE

Why not ask to look at your electricity bill at home? See if you can tell how many kilowatt hours of electricity have been used and how much each unit (kWh) costs.

CHECK YOURSELF

1 Which uses more energy, a 60 W bulb switched on for an hour or a 100 W bulb switched on for 45 minutes?

2 Work out these conversions:
   (a) How many seconds are there in an hour?
   (b) How many watts are there in a kilowatt?
   (c) Joules and kilowatt hours are both energy units. How many joules are there in a kilowatt hour?

10.5 How heat is lost at home

To stop **heat** escaping from your home, you need to understand the three ways that heat moves:

- **Conduction** – Heat flows through **solids** because the hotter particles vibrate more and pass their energy on to their neighbours.
- **Convection** – When part of a **fluid** (liquid or gas) warms up, it expands and becomes less dense; so it floats upwards, then cooler fluid moves in to take its place.
- **Radiation** – Any hot surface gives out heat energy (as **infra-red** radiation, see page 79), which can travel through air and even **empty space**.

Each type of heat loss can be stopped in different ways:

- Conduction – **Insulation foam** doesn't let the heat flow through.
- Convection – **Seal gaps** to stop the warm air from rising and leaving your house.
- Radiation – Use **shiny surfaces** to reflect the IR rays back into the house.

EXAM HINTS

Be ready to explain how insulation works and, then, to compare information about different types of insulation and say which is the best.

CHECK YOURSELF

1 Compare how heat flows through a solid to how it flows in a liquid.
2 Why do some people fix shiny foil on the walls immediately behind their radiators?
3 Explain how double-glazing helps to reduce heat loss through (a) conduction and (b) convection.

10.6 Evaluating efficiency

This **energy transfer diagram** summarises what a microwave oven does:

The energy transfer diagram shows what the **input** and **output** energy types are, as well as the waste type. You can also see what proportion of the input energy is usefully used (and how much is wasted): its **efficiency**. You can work this out using the formula:

200 J electrical energy input

130 J Heat energy in food

70 J Wasted heat and sound energy

$$efficiency = \frac{useful\ energy\ output}{total\ energy\ input}$$

(The answer is often then multiplied by 100 to give a percentage.)

You will never get an efficiency of greater than 1 (or 100 %), and rarely more than 0.5 (or 50 %).

GET IT RIGHT!

When you work out efficiency, be careful to use the useful output energy in your calculation and not the amount wasted.

AQA EXAMINER SAYS...

You can give efficiency as a decimal (between 0 and 1) or as a percentage (between 0 and 100 %), but make it really clear which one you are using.

CHECK YOURSELF

1 Draw an energy transfer diagram for a television. Remember to include input, output and waste.
2 A petrol lawnmower wastes 400 J of energy, as heat and sound, for every 500 J of chemical energy burnt. Calculate the efficiency of the lawnmower.

10.7 Improving energy efficiency

KEY POINTS

1 Improving efficiency is important for three main reasons:
- If you use less energy, you can save money.
- The non-renewable energy resources we have will last longer.
- Reducing the electricity we use will also reduce greenhouse gas emissions.
2 Efficiency is an important consideration when buying a new device.

In chapter 13 we will look at the need to find alternative energy sources because most of ours are non-renewable. If we can make our devices more efficient then our energy supplies will last for longer.

Another advantage of increased efficiency is that using less energy will save money on our electricity bills. Even though more efficient devices may often be more expensive, they should save you that extra money back in the amount of electricity they save.

Energy efficient light bulbs may be six times as expensive but:

- They last up to ten times longer.
- They use less than a third of the electricity to make the same amount of light.

An incandescent light bulb

A compact fluorescent light bulb

EXAM HINTS

When making comparisons between devices, remember to take into account the advantages and disadvantages of each type before you say that one is better than the other.

CHECK YOURSELF

1 Energy efficient light bulbs cost a lot more than filament (incandescent) light bulbs, so why can it save you money to use energy efficient bulbs?

2 If a 100 W energy efficient light bulb is 35 % efficient and a 100 W filament bulb is 10 % efficient, how much energy does each of them waste each second?

3 Explain why it is more efficient to cook vegetables with a lid on the saucepan.

Chapter 10   End of chapter questions

1 Batteries are a relatively expensive source of electricity; what are their advantages?

2 Describe the main energy transfers that take place in a stereo.

3 Which size fuse would be best for a 1500 W toaster plugged into the 230 V mains supply? 1 A, 3 A, 5 A, 10 A or 30 A.

4 A 1500 W café toaster is used for 3 hours a day. How much does this cost the café if electricity is charged for at 7 p/kW h?

5 What types of heat loss does loft insulation reduce? Describe how it does this.

6 Draw an energy transfer diagram for a filament light bulb. Include labels to show what percentage energy is transferred into each type.

7 Only about 10 % of the heat produced in a normal toaster goes to heating the bread. Suggest ways that the efficiency of the toaster could be improved.

Chapter 11 — Checklist: Useful mixtures

Tick when you:

reviewed it after your lesson	☑	☐	☐
revised once – some questions right	☑	☑	☐
revised twice – all questions right	☑	☑	☑

Move onto another topic when you have all three ticks.

Section 3 The home environment

11.1 Useful mixtures	☐	☐	☐
11.2 Mixtures in the home	☐	☐	☐
11.3 Different solvents for different jobs	☐	☐	☐
11.4 When mixtures separate	☐	☐	☐

Chapter 11 — Pre Test: Useful mixtures

1. **Name the six different types of mixture.**

2. **What do the words solute, solution, soluble and solvent mean?**

3. **What type of mixture is a jelly?**

4. **Why doesn't oil mix with water?**

5. **What types of mixture can you separate by evaporation?**

11.1 Useful mixtures

KEY POINTS

1 The six types of mixture are solutions, suspensions, aerosols, emulsions, gels and foams.
2 What's in a mixture will tell you what type of mixture it is.

What are the solvent, solute and solution here?

GET IT RIGHT!

Solvent, solution, solute and soluble are all very similar words: read questions carefully and always check your answers to make sure you haven't accidentally confused them.

We're surrounded by mixtures every day. It's actually very rare to find a completely pure substance around the home.

We can divide mixtures into different groups to help describe their properties:

Type of mixture	What's in it?	Example
Aerosol	Gas with liquid suspended in it	Deodorant spray
Emulsion	Immiscible liquids	Paint
Foam	Liquid or solid with gas bubbles inside	Whipped cream
Gel	Solid with liquid dissolved inside it	Jelly
Solution	Liquid with solute dissolved in it	Cola
Suspension	Liquid containing insoluble solid	Toothpaste

You need to be familiar with these key words when dealing with mixtures:

Solvent – a substance something can dissolve in.

Solute – a substance dissolved in a solvent.

Soluble – can dissolve in a solvent.

Insoluble – can't dissolve in a solvent.

Miscible – liquids that can mix together.

Immiscible – liquids that can't mix together.

CHECK YOURSELF

1 What type of mixture is coffee?
2 What type of mixture is the inside of a Crunchie bar?
3 What type of mixture is hairspray?

11.2 Mixtures in the home

KEY POINTS

1 Nearly every product in the kitchen or bathroom is a mixture.
2 Knowing what type of mixture something is helps you understand its properties.

CHECK YOURSELF

1 Which of the above examples contain liquids?
2 Which of the above examples could you separate easily?

Nearly everything you find at home (and especially in the kitchen or bathroom) is a mixture. Here is a selection of products you might see at home:

- Soluble aspirin – Dissolving medicine makes it easier to take.
- Toothpaste – Insoluble cellulose is mixed with water until it's thick enough to stay on your brush.
- Shaving foam – The bubbles help it hold its shape.
- Foam padding in furniture – The bubbles make it spring back into shape.
- Deodorant spray – Using gas to deliver a substance helps you choose where it goes.
- Hair gel – When the water evaporates, you're left with solid holding your hair in place.
- Mayonnaise – This is made of vinegar and oil. These don't usually mix, so egg yolk is used as an **emulsifier**. Other high-fat mixtures like chocolate also need emulsifiers to stop them separating.

Now, look back over the list at the top of the page and decide which type of mixture each product is.

11.3 Different solvents for different jobs

1 Solvents make solutes dissolve by getting between the solid particles and breaking them apart.
2 Different solvents are needed for different solutes.
3 A solvent will dissolve a substance it is chemically similar to.

Not everything dissolves in water, and there's a reason for that!

Water is a particular type of solvent – we call it an **ionic solvent**. Other ionic substances will dissolve in it, but non-ionic substances won't. This is because water is able to get between the particles of an ionic solute and break them up. If a substance is non-ionic, the water molecules just can't do much to it.

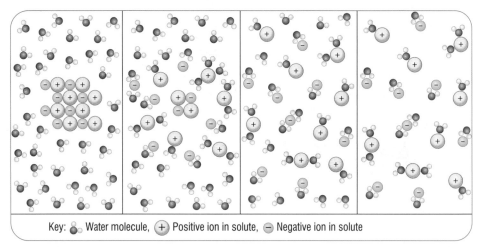

Key: ⚬ Water molecule, ⊕ Positive ion in solute, ⊖ Negative ion in solute

Solvents at work

To dissolve a **non-ionic substance**, you need a different solvent, like ethanol.

Organic solvents are very good at dissolving substances that are insoluble in water. However, they are often very dangerous. They can be flammable, cause chemical burns or even cancer.

Paints are solutions containing a coloured chemical (called a **pigment**). When the solvent dries, the pigment is left behind.

1 Look at the picture of a solute dissolving ('Solvents at work'). Describe step-by-step what is happening at each stage.

2 Why are organic solvents dangerous?

3 Why would you not use a water-soluble pigment in paint for car bodies?

GET IT RIGHT!

Remember: Not all substances dissolve in water!

11.4 When mixtures separate

KEY POINTS

1 Some mixtures can separate when left alone or exposed to the air.
2 Mixtures can be separated on purpose, by: evaporation, distillation, filtration, chromatography and sieving.

EXAM HINTS

You could be asked to use the label on a bottle to decide what type of mixture it is. Things like 'shake well before use' and 'replace cap after use' are big clues!

As well as knowing how to mix things together, we need to understand how mixtures can be separated again. This can happen two ways:

Leaving a mixture alone for a while, or exposed to the air

Suspensions are able to separate quite easily if you leave them alone for a bit. Next time you're at the supermarket, look at the orange squash. You'll see the insoluble solid has sunk down to the bottom.

Some mixtures need re-mixing

When a gas has been dissolved in a liquid, it can usually escape if the cap is left off. This is why fizzy drinks go 'flat'.

Separating things on purpose

If we want to purify things, we need to know how to separate them from whatever they're mixed with. This table shows the different separation methods we use, and when to use them:

Separation method	What can it separate?	Why does it work?
Evaporation	Solutions, suspensions, gels	The solvent has a lower boiling point than the solute or solid.
Distillation	Solutions	The solvent has a lower boiling point than the solute.
Filtration	Suspensions	Suspended solid particles are bigger than liquid particles.
Chromatography	Solutions with many solutes	Different-sized solute particles move through a material at different rates.
Sieving	Suspensions of solids	Solid particles are different sizes.

CHECK YOURSELF

1 How would you separate the solid bits from orange squash?

2 Medicines which are suspensions need to be shaken before use. Why is this really important?

3 If some ink has three different pigments in it, how could you separate them?

Chapter 11   End of chapter questions

1 Solutions and gels can both contain a solid and a liquid. How are they different?

2 Name a mixture that contains an emulsifier.

3 If a solid is insoluble in water, what other solvents could you try?

4 How could you get a pure sample of salt from a solution of salty water?

1 Limestone is major raw material and is used by many industries. It is taken from the ground in quarries. Limestone can be converted into chemicals called 'quicklime' and 'slaked lime'.

(a) Match up the material to its chemical name and formula: (6 marks)

Material	Chemical name	Formula
Limestone	Calcium hydroxide	CaO
Quicklime	Calcium oxide	$CaCO_3$
Slaked lime	Calcium carbonate	$Ca(OH)_2$

(b) Limestone can be converted to quicklime in a lime kiln:
(i) Why is this reaction described as endothermic? (1 mark)
(ii) What waste gas is produced in this process? (1 mark)

2 Metals are used by many industries because of their useful properties.
Steel is often used for car bodies. If a car body panel is knocked or dented, it can be beaten back into shape.

(a) What property of metals makes this possible? (1 mark)
(b) Describe how the structure of metallic elements makes it possible to hammer them into different shapes. (2 marks)
(c) Steel is a magnetic metal. Which magnetic element does it contain? (1 mark)

3 Materials scientists make decisions about which materials to use for which jobs. They make their decisions based on how suitable a material's properties are for different tasks.

(a) What properties would you expect porcelain to have? (4 marks)
(b) Explain how porcelain's properties make it suitable for making toilet seats from. (4 marks)

4 Emulsions are a type of mixture often found in the home. Mayonnaise and chocolate are both examples of emulsions.

(a) What are the component parts of an emulsion? (2 marks)
(b) Chocolate and mayonnaise contain a substance called an 'emulsifying agent'. What does an emulsifying agent do? (1 mark)
(c) Some salad dressings are a mixture of oil and water, and do not contain an emulsifying agent. How can you tell, by looking, that there is no emulsifying agent? (1 mark)

5 Many mixtures come with instructions to stop them separating. A bottle of medicine has the words 'shake well before use' on its label.

(a) What type of mixture might the medicine be? (1 mark)
(b) Why is it important to follow the advice on the label? (1 mark)
(c) The following diagrams show how you could separate the different substances in a mixture. Name the methods A to E. (5 marks)

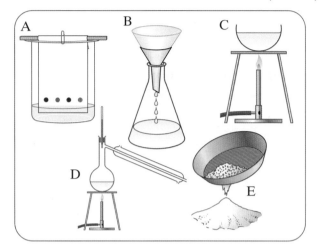

6 This table compares two bulbs of the same brightness – one is a traditional filament (incandescent) bulb and the other is an energy efficient (compact fluorescent) bulb.

An incandescent light bulb   A compact fluorescent light bulb

	Cost to buy	Power	Life	Efficiency
Filament bulb	60p	100 W	1000 hours	10 %
Energy efficient bulb	£3	25 W	10 000 hours	30 %

(a) Use the table to say which bulb:
(i) Is the cheapest.
(ii) Uses the least energy each second.
(iii) Will need replacing most often.
(iv) Has the best efficiency. (4 marks)

(b) (i) Write down the equation that links power, energy and time for an electrical device. (1 mark)
(ii) Work out how much electrical energy the filament bulb uses in an hour. (2 marks)
(iii) How much of this energy is wasted? (3 marks)

 Test & Assessment Interactive quizzes, answers and hints online!

This answer is only worth 1 mark.

The response worth a mark is underlined in red.

We can improve the answer in several ways:

An element is a substance made of one type of atom.

(a) What are the differences between an element and a compound?
(2 marks)

(b) What are the differences between a compound and a mixture?
(2 marks)

(a) The difference between an element and a compound is that an element is basically a chemical on its own, such as hydrogen and oxygen (all of the periodic table is a list of elements), but a compound is when elements are joined together, like water.

(b) The main difference between a compound and a mixture is that a compound is when two chemicals are stuck together and a mixture is usually a liquid.

A compound is when two elements are chemically joined

A mixture is two or more substances that aren't chemically joined.

The answer is worth 5 marks.
The responses worth a mark are underlined in red.
We can improve the answer:

This should read $CaCO_3$.

(a) Describe how limestone can be made into quicklime. *(3 marks)*
(b) Describe how quicklime is used to make concrete. *(3 marks)*

(a) Limestone is taken from quarries and heated very strongly in a lime kiln to produce quicklime. This also produces carbon dioxide. The chemical equation for this is:

$$CaCO_2 \rightarrow CaO + CO_2$$

(b) The quicklime is then added to clay and gypsum, which is also heated strongly. This makes cement.
Cement is added to sand, small stones and water to make concrete.

Chapter 12 — Checklist: Moving

Tick when you:

reviewed it after your lesson	☑	☐	☐
revised once – some questions right	☑	☑	☐
revised twice – all questions right	☑	☑	☑

Move onto another topic when you have all three ticks.

Section 4 Transport and communications

12.1 Vehicle velocity	☐	☐	☐
12.2 Automobile acceleration	☐	☐	☐
12.3 Stopping distances	☐	☐	☐
12.4 Safe driving	☐	☐	☐

Chapter 12 — Pre Test: Moving

1. How fast is a car travelling if it covers a distance of 500 m in 20 s?

2. A cyclist moves with a velocity of 15 m/s. How far will she travel in one minute?

3. What is the acceleration of a car that goes from 0 to 30 m/s in 15 s?

4. If a cyclist can initially accelerate at 1.5 m/s^2, how long will he take to reach a velocity of 24 m/s?

5. Write definitions for the 'thinking distance' and 'braking distance' of a car.

6. List three factors that will make braking distance increase.

7. Why is it dangerous to use a mobile phone while you are driving?

8. Why is the speed limit 70 m.p.h. on the motorways but only 30 m.p.h. in built up areas?

12.1 Vehicle velocity

1 Different vehicles travel at different speeds. Velocity is a speed in a particular direction.
2 You can work out velocity (or speed) by using the equation:

$$\text{velocity (m/s)} = \frac{\text{distance travelled (m)}}{\text{time taken (s)}}$$

3 Speed is usually measured in metres per second (m/s), but you will sometimes see it measured in miles per hour (m.p.h.) or kilometres per hour (km/h).

CHECK YOURSELF

1 A car travels 100 metres in 5 seconds. What is its speed?
2 If a cyclist was travelling at a velocity of 15 m/s, how far would she travel in 5 minutes?

Speed tells you how fast something covers a *distance*. The word '**velocity**' means almost exactly the same as speed (the only difference is that velocity describes the *direction* as well as how fast it is). Speed (and velocity) are measured in **metres per second (m/s)**.

It is worth knowing some typical speeds so that you can tell if any answers you work out are sensible:

Walking speed = 3 m/s
Motorway driving = 30 m/s
Sound (in air) = 300 m/s
Light = 300 000 000 m/s (Nothing can travel faster than light!)

To work out the velocity (or speed) of a vehicle, you need to be able to use this equation:

$$\text{velocity (m/s)} = \frac{\text{distance travelled (m)}}{\text{time taken (s)}}$$

You also need to be able to rearrange it to work out the distance travelled and time taken:

$$\text{distance travelled (m)} = \text{velocity (m/s)} \times \text{time taken (s)}$$

and:

$$\text{time taken (s)} = \frac{\text{distance travelled (m)}}{\text{velocity (m/s)}}$$

12.2 Automobile acceleration

1 'Acceleration' measures how quickly the velocity of a vehicle is changing.
2 You need to be able to use this equation to calculate acceleration:

$$\text{acceleration (m/s}^2) = \frac{\text{change in velocity (m/s)}}{\text{time taken for change(s)}}$$

3 Slowing down is called 'deceleration', and comes out as a negative acceleration.

CHECK YOURSELF

1 What are the units we normally use for distance, time, velocity and acceleration?
2 Calculate the acceleration of a runner who reaches a speed of 9 m/s in the first 2 seconds of a race.

Acceleration is a change in velocity. If a vehicle is slowing down, it is called a **deceleration**.

You can work out acceleration using this formula:

$$\text{acceleration (m/s}^2) = \frac{\text{change in velocity (m/s)}}{\text{time taken for change (s)}}$$

The units for acceleration are m/s^2 (**metres per second squared**) because that's what you get if you divide m/s (metres per second) by s (seconds).

In more difficult questions, you might be asked to work out the change in velocity, or the time taken for an acceleration. You might need to rearrange the acceleration formula to:

$$\text{change in velocity (m/s)} = \text{acceleration (m/s}^2) \times \text{time taken (s)}$$

and:

$$\text{time taken for change (s)} = \frac{\text{change in velocity (m/s)}}{\text{acceleration (m/s}^2)}$$

(The acceleration equation is only for vehicles moving in a straight line with a steady acceleration – once you start going around corners or changing the acceleration, it gets a bit more complicated.)

12.3 Stopping distances

KEY POINTS

1 The total distance a vehicle travels while it is stopping is called its stopping distance, made up of two parts:
   (a) Thinking distance – travelled before your reactions let you hit the brake.
   (b) Braking distance – travelled between hitting the brake and actually stopping.
2 The thinking distance is mainly affected by human factors – like tiredness.
3 The braking distance is mainly affected by physical factors – like road condition.

If you are driving along the road and a dog runs out in front of you, or a car in front brakes suddenly, you put your foot on the brakes – but it still takes you a while to stop:

- You travel a distance between seeing the dog and hitting the brake – this is called the **thinking distance**.
- You travel a further distance after you hit the brake until you finally stop – called the **braking distance**.

As this diagram shows, the **total stopping distance** is the sum of the thinking distance and the stopping distance:

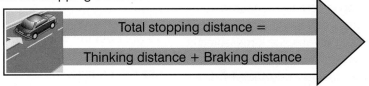

Total stopping distance =

Thinking distance + Braking distance

The faster you are travelling, the further your stopping distance will be, but other factors affect it too:

- Factors that affect your concentration affect the thinking distance – if you are tired or distracted (or if you have been drinking!).
- Factors that affect how well the brakes work affect the braking distance – like ice on the road or worn tyres.

The Highway Code

BUMP UP YOUR GRADE

The easiest way to identify which factors affect which distance is this:

Human factors, like tiredness, affect **thinking distance**.

Mechanical or physical factors, like wet roads, affect **braking distance**.

AQA EXAMINER SAYS...

Questions on this topic are about the *distances* travelled while stopping, not the time taken to stop. One reason for this is that your reaction time (your thinking time) will be the same whatever speed you are travelling at, but you will travel further in this time if you are going faster.

CHECK YOURSELF

1 Describe the worst possible combination of conditions for stopping a car quickly.

2 (a) Explain why it is important to leave a sensible gap between your car and the one in front.
   (b) Why should you leave a bigger gap when you are moving faster?

12.4 Safe driving

KEY POINTS

1 Accidents on the road cause many deaths each year. Some of the ways we try to improve road safety include:
   - the driving test
   - MOT testing for older vehicles
   - breathalysers and other measures against drink and drug drivers.
2 The Highway Code is a very useful book (and website) that contains lots of guidance about how to stay safe when using roads.

CHECK YOURSELF

1 What should a driver do on seeing each of these road safety signs?

(a) (b)

(c) (d)

2 Why shouldn't you eat or drink while you are driving?

This is how we try to make driving on the road safer:

- The **driving qualification test** has to be taken by every driver to make sure they understand the rules of the road and can handle a vehicle safely.
- Older cars have to take an **MOT test** every year, to make sure that they are safe, e.g. that their brakes and steering work well, that their tyres are safe and that they don't emit too much pollution.
- The Police can test a driver for use of **alcohol** and **drugs** if they suspect the driver of driving while under their influence.
- There are many different **road safety signs** that warn drivers about conditions ahead, as well as saying what speeds you should drive at.

In general, you must also avoid any distractions while you drive – like using a mobile phone, eating or drinking. Anything that takes your mind off the road or your hands off the controls could be dangerous.

 EXAMINER SAYS...

Questions on this topic usually need you to write sentences that give reasons for answers. You can use the empty space on the paper to make drafting notes first, like you might do in English – just cross them through to tell the examiner not to mark them.

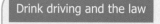

Drink driving and the law

If you are convicted of:	The maximum penalty is:
Causing death by careless driving when under the influence of drink or drugs.	14 years imprisonment, banned from driving for at least 2 years and required to take an extended driving test.
Driving or attempting to drive whilst above the legal limit or unfit through drink.	6 months imprisonment, plus a fine of £5,000 and banned from driving for at least 12 months (3 years if you're convicted twice in 10 years).
In charge of a vehicle whilst over the legal limit or unfit through drink.	3 months imprisonment, plus a fine of £2,500 and a ban from driving.
Refusing to provide a specimen of breath, blood or urine for analysis.	6 months imprisonment, plus a fine of £5,000 and banned from driving for at least 12 months.

Drink driving and the law

Chapter 12   End of chapter questions

1 A lorry travels at a speed of 25 m/s. How long will it take it to travel 5 km?

2 What is the velocity, in m/s, of a jet plane that can travel 600 km in an hour?

3 If a runner can reach a speed of 10 m/s in 2.5 s, what is her initial acceleration?

4 If a racing car can accelerate at a rate of 5 m/s^2, how fast will it be travelling after 7 s?

5 Explain why thinking distance and braking distance both increase if a car gets faster.

6 List three other factors that will cause thinking distance to increase.

7 Why does drink driving cause so many accidents?

8 Why are a car's brakes and wheels checked in its annual MOT test?

Chapter 13 — Checklist: Fuels for transport

Tick when you:

reviewed it after your lesson	☑	☐	☐
revised once – some questions right	☑	☑	☐
revised twice – all questions right	☑	☑	☑

Move onto another topic when you have all three ticks.

Section 4 Transport and communications

13.1 Burning fuels	☐	☐	☐
13.2 Engine energy and efficiency	☐	☐	☐
13.3 Transport pollution	☐	☐	☐
13.4 Alternative fuels	☐	☐	☐

Chapter 13 — Pre Test: Fuels for transport

1. Write a word equation for the combustion of a hydrocarbon.

2. How efficient is a car engine that produces 660 J of kinetic energy for every 2000 J of fuel (chemical) energy supplied?

3. Name two harmless and two harmful gases that are produced by engines.

4. What are the advantages of using alcohol (ethanol) as a fuel?

13.1 Burning fuels

Crude oil is a mixture of lots of organic molecules, called **hydrocarbons**, of different lengths.

One family of hydrocarbons is the **alkanes** – methane, ethane, propane, butane, pentane. . . and so on.

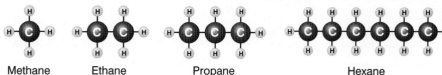

Methane   Ethane   Propane   Hexane

When these fuels burn, or **combust**, they react with the oxygen in the air as shown by this **word equation**:

$$\text{hydrocarbon} + \text{oxygen} \rightarrow \text{carbon dioxide} + \text{water}$$

You also need to be able to write the **symbol equations** for hydrocarbon combustion, like this one for propane:

$$C_3H_8 + 5O_2 \rightarrow 3CO_2 + 4H_2O$$

The longer hydrocarbon molecules release more energy when they are burnt. This is why heavier vehicles like jumbo jets burn hydrocarbons with longer molecules than cars do.

An oil refinery

CHECK YOURSELF

1 What two gases are always produced when hydrocarbons burn?

2 Which two fractions of crude oil are most commonly used to fuel cars?

3 What is the link between the length of a hydrocarbon molecule and the amount of energy it can release?

13.2 Engine energy and efficiency

This energy transfer diagram shows what happens in an engine:

100% Fuel energy (combustion)

25% Effective power: movement and accessories

5% Friction losses

30% Coolant

40% Exhaust gas

The proportion of energy that the engine can use usefully is called its **efficiency**. You can work out efficiency using this formula:

$$\text{efficiency} = \frac{\text{useful energy output}}{\text{total energy input}}$$

(You can multiply the answer by 100 to get a %)

Most engines are only about 30% efficient, so 70% of the fuel put into them is wasted! Engine designers are always trying to make more efficient engines. Not only will this save money, but it will make our petrol last longer (and cause less pollution, too!)

GET IT RIGHT!

Efficiency can be stated either as a percentage or as a decimal (between 0 and 1).

13.3 Transport pollution

When not enough oxygen gets into the engine for all of the fuel to fully combust, the result is **incomplete combustion**. This wastes energy and causes pollution, too.

One of the main products of complete combustion (see page 75) is carbon dioxide. With incomplete combustion, **carbon monoxide** is made instead – this is poisonous.

Engines also produce other pollution: VOCs and NO_x can cause health problems as well as adding to the effects of **acid rain**. Any impurities in the fuel also burn and can produce soot.

Most modern cars have **catalytic converters** fitted to make these gases safer. Older cars have their exhaust gases monitored as part of their MOT tests.

GET IT RIGHT!

Think about the main differences between complete and incomplete combustion. When there isn't enough oxygen, carbon monoxide is formed instead of carbon dioxide.

13.4 Alternative fuels

KEY POINTS

1 We need alternative fuels for our vehicles because:
  • Petrol and diesel come from crude oil, which will run out.
  • They cause pollution.
2 Alternatives for powering cars include alcohol, hydrogen combustion, electric cars and hydrogen fuel cells.

Most **fuels** that are used in transport come from **crude oil**, including:

• petrol or gasoline – car fuel
• paraffin, kerosene – jet fuel
• diesel oil, gas oil – used by some cars and larger vehicles.

We need to be developing **alternative fuels** to take over because fossil fuels are non-renewable and cause too much pollution.

There are several alternative fuels in different stages of development at the moment, such as:

• **Hydrogen** – This can be burnt as a fuel or used in fuel cells to generate electricity. Either way, the storage of large amounts of hydrogen in a small vehicle is a problem.
• **Alcohol** (or gasohol) – This is produced by fermenting sugars. Ethanol burns cleanly (except for the production of carbon dioxide) and is completely renewable.
• **Electric** cars – They run on banks of rechargeable batteries, but the batteries are heavy and take a long time to charge up. However, research continues to improve batteries. We have also developed 'hybrid' cars that can switch between running on petrol and electricity.

An electric car

A hydrogen fuelled car

Chapter 13   End of chapter questions

1 **Write a symbol equation for the combustion of methane (CH_4).**

2 **Name three different fractions of crude oil and explain what each is used for.**

3 **Describe how car engines waste as much energy as they do.**

4 **Why is an 'emissions test' an important part of MOT testing?**

Chapter 14 — Checklist: Communications

Tick when you:

reviewed it after your lesson ☑ ☐ ☐

revised once – some questions right ☑ ☑ ☐

revised twice – all questions right ☑ ☑ ☑

Move onto another topic when you have all three ticks.

Section 4 Transport and communications

14.1 Introduction to electromagnetic waves ☐ ☐ ☐

14.2 Communicating with waves ☐ ☐ ☐

14.3 Properties of electromagnetic waves ☐ ☐ ☐

14.4 Properties of electromagnetic waves – 2 ☐ ☐ ☐

14.5 Looking out into the Universe ☐ ☐ ☐

14.6 The Universe is getting bigger! ☐ ☐ ☐

Chapter 14 — Pre Test: Communications

1. List the seven main types of electromagnetic wave.

2. How are microwaves used in communication?

3. Describe how X-rays can be: (a) useful and (b) harmful.

4. Why do some people think that the microwaves used for mobile phone transmissions might be dangerous?

5. Why do some astronomers use radio telescopes?

6. How do most scientists think the Universe began?

14.1 Introduction to electromagnetic waves

KEY POINTS

1 The colours of light that we can see are only part of a bigger family of waves, called the **electromagnetic spectrum**.
2 All of these waves travel at the same speed through air (and space), i.e. at 300 000 000 m/s.
3 Each type of electromagnetic wave has a different frequency, measured in Hertz (Hz), which shows many waves are produced each second.
4 Higher frequency waves also have a higher energy, which means that they have different properties, so each wave can be used for different things.

EXAM HINTS

One of the most common questions on this topic asks you to put the electromagnetic waves in the right order: so try to learn it. Pick an end to start at, say the low frequency end, and practise getting the order right.

- **Waves** carry energy from one place to another, as **vibrations**.
- The number of vibrations of a wave in each second is called its **frequency** and is measured in **Hertz** (Hz).
- One very important family of waves is called the **electromagnetic spectrum**.

All of these waves travel at the same speed (an amazing 300 000 000 m/s!) through air, and even through empty space. However, they all have different **wavelengths** and **frequencies**, which affect their properties and so what they can be used for. For example:

- **Visible light** is the type of electromagnetic wave that you will know best: it has its own spectrum (remember ROYGBIV?).

- **Infra-red** waves have a lower energy than visible light: they are given off by anything that is hot.

- **Ultra-violet** waves have a higher energy than visible light and are the part of sunlight that give you a tan.

- A key idea is that higher frequency waves have more energy and this affects what they are used for, as well as how dangerous they can be.

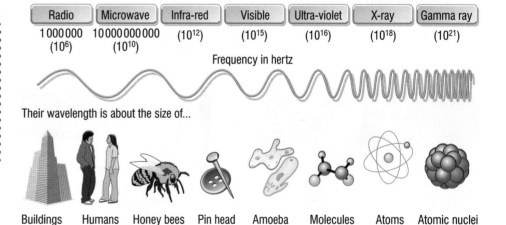

The electromagnetic spectrum

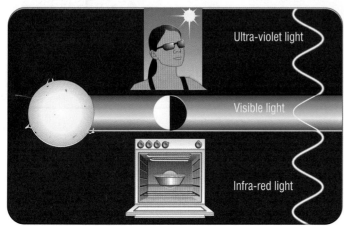

The visible light spectrum between UV and IR

CHECK YOURSELF

1 Compare radio waves and gamma waves:
   (a) Which has the longest wavelength?
   (b) Which has the highest frequency?
   (c) Which has the most energy?
   (d) Which travels the fastest?

2 What are the units for energy, wavelength, frequency and wave speed?

Communicating with waves

KEY POINTS

1 Many different types of waves are used for communications, because they carry energy from one place to another.
2 Most of the lower energy electromagnetic waves are used for communication:
   - **Radio waves** are used for television and radio transmissions.
   - **Microwaves** are used for mobile phone and satellite communications.
   - **Infra-red** waves are used for short distance communication, like wireless computer links and remote controls.
   - **Visible light** is used in optical fibres.

We can control the ways that different waves **vibrate**, e.g. by carefully varying their **frequency** (called FM, for frequency modulation). As a result, information can be coded into waves that are transmitted; in other words, we can use them for communication.

The **wavelength** and frequency of a wave affect how much information it can hold, and how far it can be sent. A rough rule is that longer wavelengths can travel further, but can't hold as much information as higher frequency waves.

Here are some examples:

High frequency ↕ Low frequency	Short wavelength ↕ Long wavelength	Infra-red	Short distance remote controls and wireless computer links
		Microwaves	Medium range and direct line mobile phone and satellite communications
		Radio waves	Long distance radio and television transmissions

Optical fibres can carry light (including **infra-red**) very long distances by reflecting it along the inside of a glass cable, e.g. for cable TV and broadband, or for use in **endoscopes**.

A mobile phone mast

Surgeons use endoscopes in keyhole surgery

BUMP UP YOUR GRADE

Think about how your remote control works. Can you get it to reflect off a wall, the ceiling or a mirror? Will it work through a door, a curtain or a piece of paper? This tells you a lot about how IR can be used in communication.

CHECK YOURSELF

1 Describe two different uses of radio waves.

2 How is infra-red radiation used for 'night vision'?

KEY POINTS

1 The wavelength of a wave gets shorter as its frequency (and energy) increase.
2 The properties of a wave depend on its wavelength and frequency: different waves can be reflected, absorbed or transmitted by different materials.
3 Waves with a high frequency or energy can be harmful, so we have to be careful with their use.

BUMP UP YOUR GRADE

Learn the scientific words to use here, e.g. reflect, transmit, absorb, fluoresce etc. You could make your own glossary of useful words as you go through revising.

CHECK YOURSELF

1 Describe one surface that reflects visible light, one that absorbs it and one that transmits it.

2 Compare X-rays to microwaves: how are they similar and how are they different?

3 Describe how fluorescent marker pens can be used for security marking of your property.

4 Say whether each of these pairs is proportional or inversely proportional:

(a) energy and frequency

(b) energy and wavelength

(c) frequency and wavelength.

5 'Gamma rays can be used to treat cancers, but they can also cause cancers.' Explain how these two statements can both be true.

There are two main patterns that you need to know about that affect the properties of waves:

- Higher **frequency** electromagnetic waves have more **energy**.
- Higher frequency waves also have a shorter **wavelength**.

So, for example:

- **Gamma rays** have a very high energy and frequency, but a very short wavelength.
- **Radio waves** have wavelengths bigger than houses, or even mountains!

When a wave hits a surface, like a window, there are three different things it could do:

- **Reflect** – The wave could bounce back off the surface.
- **Transmit** – The wave could pass straight through the surface and come out the other side.
- **Absorb** – The energy of the wave could get 'soaked' up into the surface.

An important thing to realise is that different waves react differently on different surfaces. For example:

- A brick wall will *reflect* visible light, but will *transmit* radio waves – they will just pass straight through it.
- **X-rays** can pass (transmit) through your skin and muscles, but not your bones – so doctors use them to diagnose broken bones.
- **Microwaves** of a very specific frequency get absorbed by water and heat it up, but microwaves of other frequencies pass straight through without having an effect. (Think about the different properties needed for mobile phone microwaves, compared to those used in microwave ovens.)
- **Fluorescent** materials can absorb **ultra-violet** waves and then give the energy back out as visible light, so that they glow in the dark.
- Some frequencies of radio waves can reflect off water and solid objects, so they are used for **radar** detection. (In fact, some can pass through clouds and some can't, so you have to pick the right frequency for the use you need.)

Don't forget that all of this communication technology can have a huge impact on our society and environment. Just think about the mobile phone transmission masts that are appearing all over the place; many people think that they are ugly and some people believe that they could be causing harm to people nearby.

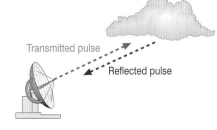

Transmitted pulse

Reflected pulse

Transmitted radio waves being reflected off clouds

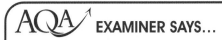 **EXAMINER SAYS...**

Make sure you include enough detail when you answer questions about uses of waves. Don't just say that 'X-rays are used to take X-rays', or that 'microwaves are used in microwaves', *explain how* they are used.

KEY POINTS

1 Although other planets, stars and galaxies are too far away for us to visit, light from them is reaching us all of the time.
2 In fact, all types of electromagnetic waves are arriving from space and they can tell us a lot about what happens out there.
3 Astronomers use a wide range of different types of telescopes to detect these electromagnetic waves and learn about space.

Radio waves are used to communicate with the robotic probes that we have been sending out to Mars, Venus and further out into the Solar System for more than 30 years. We send robots because these distances are too far to send people safely.

Even radio waves, travelling millions of times faster than we could ever travel in rockets, take hours to cross the Solar System. It would take us many thousands of years to visit even the nearest other star.

As well as being a long way away, the Sun is far too hot for us to ever visit. As well as all the visible light, it emits huge amounts of IR waves, UV waves, X-rays and radio waves.

So, although we'll never visit most of these places, we can still study them by detecting and analysing the electromagnetic waves that travel through space to us from them. Many astronomers don't use traditional 'optical' **telescopes** to look at visible light anymore. Instead they use:

- **Radio telescopes** to detect radio waves from distant objects (as well as looking for signs of intelligent life out there).
- **Microwave imaging** to look at the surface of Venus through its clouds.
- **Infra-red imaging** to look at the heat given off by different planets and moons.
- **X-ray** and **gamma-ray** cameras to detect high energy objects like neutron stars and even black holes.
- Computers then 'translate' these detected waves into visible light images that can be studied.

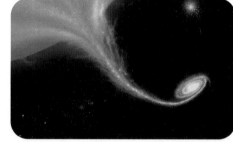

Gas from a star spiralling into a black hole (giving out gamma rays). This is a computer graphic, not an actual photo.

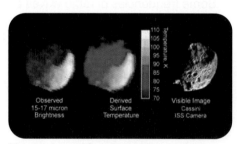

Phoebe (one of Saturn's moons (visible and IR))

CHECK YOURSELF

1 We can see that the Sun gives out lots of light, how can we tell that it also emits ultra-violet and infra-red radiations?
2 How many of each of the following are there in our Solar System:
   (a) planets
   (b) stars
   (c) galaxies?
3 Why can't we look at gamma rays and radio waves through normal 'optical' telescopes?

14.6 The Universe is getting bigger!

KEY POINTS

1 Most scientists believe that the Universe began with a huge explosion (the Big Bang) and is still expanding today.
2 There are two main pieces of strong evidence for the Big Bang theory:
   - **Galactic red-shift** tells us all distant galaxies are heading away from us.
   - **Microwave radiation** in space could be the left over heat from the explosion.

BUMP UP YOUR GRADE

When writing about the Big Bang theory, try to remember that it is just the best theory that we have at the moment. We can't say it's a *fact*, because no one was there to see it happen, but we can definitely say that there is some very strong *evidence* that supports the theory.

GET IT RIGHT!

When talking about red-shift, remember to get the scale right and say that it is *galaxies* that are moving away from us, not stars or planets.

A very important theory that astronomers have come up with from observations of electromagnetic waves from space is the **Big Bang** theory. This states that the **Universe** started with a huge explosion.

There are two main pieces of evidence for this theory that can be compared to any explosion, i.e. explosions make things hot and send things flying outwards. Let's look at the evidence and what it means:

How is an explosion like the Big Bang?

- Wherever astronomers look in the night sky, they detect some low level energy at **microwave** frequencies. Is this the **radiation** left over from a huge explosion?
- The light from distant galaxies is 'stretched out' to longer wavelengths than we would expect. This '**red-shift**' (red is a longer wavelength than blue) of the light is what would happen if those galaxies were *moving away* from us. As well as this, astronomers have detected larger red-shifts in galaxies that are further away, so those ones are moving even faster away from us.

So there is leftover heat and things spreading outwards. This is just what you would expect if the Universe started with a Big Bang!

CHECK YOURSELF

1 Explain how these two pieces of evidence lead scientists to believe that the Universe began with a 'Big Bang':

   (a) galactic red-shift

   (b) cosmic microwave background radiation.

2 Which of the types of evidence named in question 1 could be detected with an optical telescope and which would need a radio telescope? Explain your answers.

Chapter 14   End of chapter questions

1 **List all of the parts of the electromagnetic spectrum in order, from lowest energy to highest.**

2 **Draw a diagram to show the differences between reflection, transmission and absorption of waves.**

3 **Describe how gamma rays can be (a) useful and (b) harmful.**

4 **What types of electromagnetic wave can we detect from the surface of Venus?**

5 **What does the red-shift of light from distant galaxies tell us?**

1 This table shows manufacturers' information about the cars they produce. Use this information to answer the following questions.

Car make	Acceleration (0-60 m.p.h)	Top speed	Fuel consumption
Vauxhall Astra	13.50 s	172 km/h	61.41 m.p.g.
Ford Focus	12.50 s		51.36 m.p.g.
Nissan Almera	10.80 s	185 km/h	37.66 m.p.g.
Ford Puma	8.80 s	203 km/h	38.17 m.p.g.

(a) (i) Describe the link between the acceleration of the cars and their top speed. (1 mark)

(ii) Which car could travel the furthest in an hour? (1 mark)

(iii) Estimate the top speed of the Ford Focus. (1 mark)

(iv) At its top speed, how far could the Nissan Almera travel in half an hour? (3 marks)

(b) 60 m.p.h. is the same as 27 m/s.

(i) Calculate the acceleration of the Vauxhall Astra, in m/s^2, as it accelerates from 0 to 60 m.p.h. (3 marks)

(ii) Is the Vauxhall Astra the most efficient of these cars – or is it the least efficient? Explain your answer. (2 marks)

2 This chart shows how the electricity generated by renewable resources in the United Kingdom has changed between 1998 and 2004:

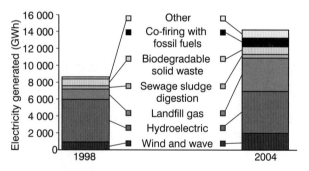

(a) (i) What does the word 'renewable' mean? (1 mark)

(ii) Why is important that our use of renewable resources keeps increasing? (2 marks)

(b) (i) Which resource has remained the UK's main renewable source of electricity? (1 mark)

(ii) Which resource has increased the most in use between 1998 and 2004? (1 mark)

(iii) The resource in part (ii) is renewable but it does have disadvantages. Name and describe one of these disadvantages. (2 marks)

(c) Wind and wave power are grouped together in this chart. Explain what these two resources have in common. (2 marks)

3 This diagram shows how far different electromagnetic waves from space travel through the atmosphere. Read the article below about how this affects the work of astronomers.

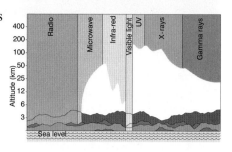

Look up into the sky at night and it seems that the atmosphere is transparent – that light from distant stars can reach us on the ground. But remember, visible light is just one part of the electromagnetic spectrum. Only a very few wavelengths, such as the visible spectrum, radio frequencies and some ultra-violet wavelengths can travel all the way through the atmosphere. To most of the other parts of the spectrum, the atmosphere is opaque!

This can be a problem for astronomers because it means there is a lot of information coming from space that they can't see. But astronomers are determined people – to see infra-red rays from space, they go to mountain tops or fly their telescopes in aircraft. Balloons can carry sensors up to 30 km high to carry out experiments lasting months. Rockets can be used to take experiments up to the edge of space – but these fall back to Earth, so the experiments can't last long. The best way to detect every type of electromagnetic wave coming from space is to put your detectors on a satellite!

(a) This table summarises some of the information in the article. Copy the table.

Type of wave	Energy of wave	Transmitted or absorbed by atmosphere	Where detectors/telescopes can be
Radio			Ground
Microwave	Low	Absorbed (some transmitted)	Aircraft
Infra-red	Medium	Absorbed	Mountains/aircraft
Visible		Transmitted	
Ultra-violet	Medium	Absorbed (some transmitted)	Satellite
X-rays	High		
Gamma rays		Absorbed	Satellite

(i) Complete the 'Energy of wave' column, using the words: **low**, **medium** or **high**. (2 marks)

(ii) Fill in the two gaps in the 'Transmitted or absorbed' column. (2 marks)

(iii) Look at the diagram and decide where the best places would be to detect visible light and X-rays from. Write your answers into the table. (2 marks)

(b) (i) Which type of electromagnetic wave does the atmosphere block the most? (1 mark)

(ii) Why can astronomers detect infra-red rays on mountain tops, but not at sea level? (1 mark)

(c) The article says that the best way to detect every type of wave is to use a satellite. Explain two disadvantages of doing this. (2 marks)

This answer is worth 6 marks. The responses worth a mark are underlined in red. We can improve the answer in several ways:

This is a two-mark question – it needs more than this!

Your answer should be about stopping distances. **You are more likely to need to stop suddenly on single carriageways, so you need to travel slower to have a shorter stopping distance.**

m.p.h. – remember the units!

This is set out perfectly! With the equation first, then with the numbers put in and finally the answer has the right units. Being careful and thorough like this means that you are less likely to make mistakes.

This chart is from a government report on speeding vehicles. It shows the percentage of each type of vehicle that travels faster than the speed limit on different types of road.

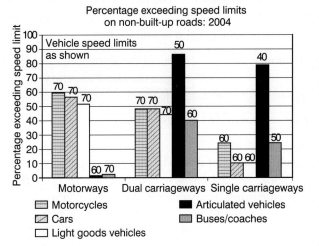

(a) (i) Complete these sentences by filling in the gaps with the types of road from the chart:
Articulated vehicles speed most on ..., but very little on ....
Smaller vehicles break the speed limit most on ...   *(3 marks)*

(ii) Why do you think the speed limits on single carriageways are lower than on motorways?   *(2 marks)*

(b) (i) Use the chart to determine the speed limit for articulated vehicles on motorways.
   (1 marks)

(ii) How long would it take an articulated vehicle to travel the 300 miles from Birmingham to Edinburgh, travelling at this speed?   *(2 marks)*

(iii) How much longer would it take to travel this distance on single carriageway roads, keeping to the speed limit?

(a) (i) Articulated vehicles speed most on <u>dual carriageways</u>, but very little on <u>motorways</u>.
Smaller vehicles break the speed limit most on motorways.
(ii) So cars don't travel as <u>fast.</u>
(b) (i) 60
(ii) time = <u>distance ÷ speed</u> = 300 / 60 = <u>5 hours</u>
(iii) time = distance ÷ speed = 300 / 40 = 7.5 hours

Oops! You forgot to work out the **extra time** that was asked for in the question, i.e. 7.5 – 5 = 2.5 hours longer.

Paper 1 (30 marks)

1 (a) Doctors and scientists are constantly warning us about the dangers of smoking. The three main components of tobacco smoke are listed below. Match the component to the damaging effect it has on the body. (3 marks)

Nicotine	Reduces the amount of oxygen the blood can carry.
Tar	Addictive.
Carbon monoxide	Causes cancer.

(b) What is a drug? (1 mark)

(c) Alcohol is another drug which people commonly consume. Which body system does it affect? (1 mark)

(d) If people drink large amounts of alcohol over a period of time they become addicted. If they try to give up they suffer from unpleasant side effects like shaking. What name is given to these conditions? (1 mark)

2 Dieticians advise everyone to eat a healthy diet. You should carefully read the labels on your food to monitor what you are eating. This label is taken from a yoghurt.

Nutritional information	Typical values per 100 g
Energy	425 kJ
Protein	6 g
Carbohydrate	12.5 g
(of which sugars)	12 g
Fat	3.9 g
(of which saturates)	2.6 g
Fibre	0.4 g
Sodium	0.1 g

(a) What mass of salt is found in 100 g of yoghurt? (1 mark)

(b) What mass of sugar would you consume if you ate a 125 g pot of yoghurt? (1 mark)

(c) Copy and complete the table below. (3 marks)

Food group	Role in the body
	Store of energy, keep you warm and covers your vital organs, protecting them from damage.
	Main source of energy.
	Building and repairing cells.

(d) Explain why eating too much saturated fat is bad for you. (3 marks)

3 (a) Microorganisms play an important role in the production of a number of food and drink products. Match the microorganism to the products it is involved in making: (2 marks)

Yeast	bread
	cheese
Bacteria	yoghurt
	wine

(b) To make beer, brewers add yeast to the malt. What process does the yeast carry out to turn this into alcohol? (1 mark)

(c) As well as producing alcohol, what gas is also made by this process? (1 mark)

(d) Describe simply how yoghurt is made. (4 mark)

4 (a) The most common way for you to 'catch' a disease is through contact with an infected person, or by being exposed to unhygienic conditions. Copy and complete the table to show how you can protect yourself from infectious diseases: (3 marks)

Protection method	Method of spread	Example of a disease this offers protection against
Covering your mouth and nose		Flu
	Through body fluids exchanged during sexual intercourse	Syphilis
Using new sterilised needles	Through blood	

(b) Doctors strongly advise that children should be immunised against certain diseases. Name a disease that most children are immunised against. (1 mark)

(c) Why do immunisations not make you ill, even though they contain microorganisms? (1 mark)

(d) Immunisations work by 'tricking' your white blood cells into causing an immune response. Describe how an immunisation causes immunity. (3 marks)

Paper 2 (38 marks)

1 This is a table of information about the group of chemicals called the alkanes:

Name	Molecular formula	Boiling point (°C)	State at 25°C
methane	CH_4	–164	gas
ethane	C_2H_6	–89	
propane	C_3H_8	–42	
butane	C_4H_{10}	–0.5	
pentane	C_5H_{12}	36	liquid
hexane	C_6H_{14}	69	

(a) The final column of the table is incomplete. Fill in the states of the alkanes at 25°C.   (3 marks)

(b) Name the two elements that make up all of the alkanes.   (2 marks)

(c) When the alkanes burn in air, they react with oxygen in a chemical reaction, part of which is shown here:
      alkane + oxygen   … + …
   (i) What is the name given to this reaction? (1 mark)
   (ii) What are the names of the two chemicals produced in this reaction?   (2 marks)

(d) Which alkane releases the most energy when it is burned? Explain your answer.   (2 marks)

2 At a speed of 30 m/s, the thinking distance for a car is 20 m and its braking distance is 75 m.

(a) (i) What is meant by the terms 'thinking distance' and 'braking distance'?   (2 marks)
    (ii) What is the overall stopping distance for the car at 30 m/s?   (1 mark)

(b) (i) Write down the equation that links distance travelled to speed and time taken.   (1 mark)
    (ii) How long does the car take to travel the 20 m thinking distance?   (2 marks)

(c) (i) Write down the equation that links acceleration to change in speed and time taken for that change.   (1 mark)
    (ii) Once the brakes are activated, the car actually takes 5 s to come to a stop. Calculate its deceleration while braking.   (2 marks)

3 Information can be communicated in many different ways. The following table contains information about four ways.

	Approximate speed ( )	Range	Device
Sound	330		
Radiowaves	300 000 000		
Fibre optics	200 000 000	Hundreds of miles	LED
Phone signal	100 000 000		

(a) (i) The units are missing from the approximate speed column. What are they?   (1 mark)
    (ii) Here are words to describe the range of each of the communication methods. Copy them into the empty spaces in a copy of the table in the correct order:
Across a field   Across the Solar System   Around the world
           (2 marks)
    (iii) Each type of signal is produced by a different device. Complete the last column of the table with devices from this list.
Megaphone   Microphone   Transmitter
           (2 marks)

(b) There are now nearly as many mobile phones in the UK as there are land lines.
   (i) Explain why there are some health concerns over the use of mobile phones.   (2 marks)
   (ii) Give one other disadvantage and one advantage of mobile phones, compared to land lines.   (2 marks)

4 Look at this table. It contains information about the hydrocarbon family called 'alkanes'.

Name	Molecular formula	Melting point (°C)	Boiling point (°C)	Energy released on combustion (kJ)
Methane	CH_4	–182	–162	889
Ethane	C_2H_6	–183	–88.6	1557
Propane	C_3H_8	–188	–42.1	2217
Butane	C_4H_{10}	–138	–0.5	2874
Pentane	C_5H_{12}	–130	36.1	3536

(a) (i) Most of these alkanes are gases at room temperature. Explain how this can be known from the table.   (2 marks)
    (ii) Which of the alkanes listed here is not a gas at room temperature? Explain your answer.
           (2 marks)

(b) This is the chemical equation for the combustion of ethane: $2C_2H_6 + 7O_2 \rightarrow 4CO_2 + 6H_2O$
   (i) The chemical formula for ethane is C_2H_6. What are the names of the elements that make up ethane?   (2 marks)
   (ii) Name the two chemicals that are produced in this reaction.   (2 marks)

(c) If there isn't enough oxygen available for complete combustion of the alkanes, other products like soot and carbon monoxide are formed. These chemical equations show two possible outcomes for the incomplete combustion of methane:

$$2CH_4 + 3O_2 \rightarrow 2CO + 4H_2O$$
$$CH_4 + O_2 \rightarrow C + 2H_2O$$

(i) What is the chemical formula for carbon monoxide? (1 mark)

(ii) What is the chemical formula for soot? (1 mark)

Paper 3 (30 marks)

1 The petrochemical industry is involved in crude oil and its products. Crude oil is a mixture of compounds containing hydrogen and carbon (hydrocarbons).

6
C
12

1
H
1

(a) How many protons are there in a carbon atom? (1 mark)

(b) How many electrons are there in a hydrogen atom? (1 mark)

(c) As well as protons and electrons, what other particles are found in carbon atoms? (1 mark)

(d) What is the charge of (i) a proton and (ii) an electron? (2 marks)

(e) In hydrocarbons, carbon and hydrogen atoms share electrons. What is this type of bonding called? (1 mark)

(f) Hydrocarbons are pumped out of the Earth as a mixture. Describe how they are separated. (2 marks)

(g) Name two materials we can use straight from the ground without having to separate them. (2 marks)

2 Lead is mined from the ground as an ore. In this form, lead atoms are chemically bonded to oxygen atoms to form lead oxide.

(a) What is the name given to two or more atoms joined together by chemical bonds? (1 mark)

(b) Lead ore is reduced to produce lead. Which reducing agent is used? (1 mark)

(c) Lead is said to be very dense. What does this mean in terms of its particles? (1 mark)

(d) What is the chemical formula for lead oxide? (1 mark)

(e) Describe two of the environmental effects of mining lead ore from the Earth. (4 marks)

3 Composites are specialist materials that combine two or more substances.

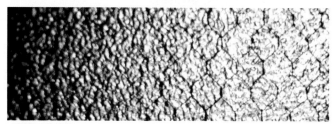

Reinforced glass

A composite material can be made by reinforcing glass with metal wires. This makes the glass less likely to shatter when hit.

(a) Describe and explain the properties of metals and glass that are exploited in using reinforced glass for windows. (4 marks)

(b) Name a composite material that could be used to make speedboats. (1 mark)

4

This powdered flu remedy needs to be mixed with hot water to make a flu remedy drink.

(a) Match up these words to the different substances in a cup of flu remedy: (3 marks)

Powdered flu remedy		Solvent
Hot water		Solute
Flu remedy drink		Solution

(b) Explain why water is able to dissolve the powdered flu remedy. (2 marks)

(c) Describe how you could separate the water and the flu remedy once they are mixed. (2 marks)

Exam preparation

Taking your Applied Science Unit 2 exam might seem a bit daunting – it doesn't have to be!

The key to performing well in your exam is to *stay calm* and *be prepared*.

Be prepared!

Start early – the more time you give yourself to get ready for the exam, the easier it's going to be. Give yourself *at least* a month to go over Unit 2. You don't want to be panicking the night before the exam!

Make a revision timetable

Plan your timetable well – make it realistic – don't say you're going to get through three chapters per night if you know it'll overload you. Don't forget to add plenty of breaks!

Stick to your timetable

There's no point making one if you don't! Plan to have finished revising the unit with a week left to spare before the exam. Spend the last week going over the topics that need more work.

Record your revision

- Very few people can revise by just reading a book. Use this revision guide to test yourself – it's *full* of questions to get you thinking.

- Use notepads, cards, sticky notes to record the key points about each topic.

- If you have friends doing the same exam, try revising together. You could even text each other questions to test each other.

Practise the exam

- This book has lots of practice questions for each topic. There are also practice exam papers for you to try.

- As well as the questions in this book, you can find sample exam material on the AQA website at www.aqa.org.uk. Try as many as you can to get a feel for the type of questions you might be asked.

- Use the mark schemes to find out how to improve your scores.

Stay calm!

- The night before the exam, make sure you have a balanced meal and an early night.

- Cramming all through the night will just tire you out and make you underperform.

- Check you've already packed everything you'll need for the exam the night before – avoid rushing around in the morning!

- Don't forget to have something sensible to eat on the day of the exam. Your brain needs nutrients to function at its best. A bottle of water will also help you concentrate in the exam.

- On the way to the exam, go over the names of the topics you have studied. Try to remember a few key facts about each of them. Revision cards help here.

Once you're in the exam

So you're about to go into the exam. You've had one last look at your notes; you've checked your equipment; you're ready. . .

(Yes, you've been told this hundreds of times, but it really does make a difference!)

- Read the question thoroughly. If it starts with some information – *read it!* Don't just jump straight in.

- Pace yourself. The questions will get harder towards the end of the exam.

- Look at the marks given for each answer. Use this to decide how much time to spend on the question.

- Relax. You won't function well if you're full of adrenaline.

Answers to questions

Chapter 1

Pre Test

1 To absorb light energy needed for photosynthesis. **2** By diffusion. **3** Respiration. **4** Three of: red blood cell, white blood cell, nerve cell, root hair cell etc. **5** To deliver oxygen to your cells. **6** Carbon dioxide is exchanged for oxygen. **7** Sensory, relay and motor neurones. **8** Hormonal responses are slower, longer lasting and act over a larger area than nervous responses. **9** As the water from sweat evaporates on the surface of your skin, it takes heat energy from the body making you feel cooler. **10** Three of: eye colour, natural hair colour, blood group and the presence of a genetic disorder. **11** DNA. **12** Different forms of the same gene.

Check yourself

1.1

1 It contains the information that determines the appearance and function of a cell and the information needed to make new cells. **2** In the mitochondria. **3** To provide structure and support.

1.2

1 Only some molecules can pass through it. **2** Particles move from a place of high concentration to a place of low concentration.

1.3

1 glucose + oxygen → carbon dioxide + water + **energy** **2** Your muscle cells need lots of energy for movement etc. This is produced by respiration in the mitochondria.

1.4

1 It contains haemoglobin and has no nucleus and a disc-like shape to increase its surface area for carrying oxygen. **2** To absorb water and nutrients from the soil. **3** It contains lots of chloroplasts and is long and thin, to produce a large surface area for absorbing light for photosynthesis.

1.5

1 Oxygenated blood is oxygen-rich whereas deoxygenated blood contains low levels of oxygen. **2** Digested food, waste e.g. carbon dioxide, hormones, blood cells and antibodies. **3** Left ventricle→body→right atrium→right ventricle→lungs→left atrium→left ventricle.

1.6

1 A sheet of muscle that moves up and down altering the volume of the thorax. **2** In-between your ribs. **3** Inhaled air contains high levels of oxygen and low levels of carbon dioxide compared with exhaled air.

1.7

1 Detect stimuli in your environment and change the stimulus into electrical impulses. **2** Central nervous system.

1.8

1 Three of: insulin, glucagons, oestrogen, testosterone, adrenaline, etc. **2** In glands.

1.9

1 37°C. **2** Hairs on your skin lie flat, sweat glands produce sweat and blood vessels near the surface of your skin widen. **3** The rapid muscle contractions require extra energy, so your cells respire more producing extra heat.

1.10

1 Differences within members of a species. **2** Three of: hair colour, eye colour, height, intelligence, hair length. **3** Both: height is influenced by your parents, but if you don't eat a proper diet you will not grow as tall as you are capable of, etc.

1.11

1 23 **2** 46 **3** A section of DNA that codes for one characteristic.

1.12

1 Dominant genes are always expressed if present in a nucleus, whereas recessive genes will only be expressed if you have two copies of them. **2** Brown hair gene, blonde hair gene, black hair gene.

End of chapter questions

1 Nucleus, cell membrane, cytoplasm and mitochondria. **2** Water molecules. **3** Water and carbon dioxide. **4** A cell that is adapted to perform a specific function. **5** Arteries, veins and capillaries. **6** The diaphragm contracts and moves down and the intercostal muscles move the ribs up and out. This increases the volume of the thorax and air is drawn in. **7** The receptor cells detect a stimulus and change it to an electrical impulse that travels along a sensory neurone to the CNS. The brain decides how to respond and sends a message via a motor neurone to a muscle or gland that causes an effect. **8** To regulate blood sugar levels. **9** Hairs on your skin stand on end; sweat glands do not produce sweat and blood vessels near the surface of your skin narrow. **10** Three of: feather colour, beak length, wing span, height. **11** Through his sperm. **12** Black – it is the dominant gene.

Chapter 2

Pre Test

1 A bacterium has a cell wall and genetic material that floats around in the cytoplasm, whereas a virus is smaller, has a protein coat and only a few genes that float about inside the virus. **2** (a) Covering your mouth and nose with a mask/handkerchief. (b) Not touching infected people or objects they have contaminated. **3** By making antibodies, which destroy microorganisms, and anti-toxins, which destroy the toxins that some microorganisms make. **4** For building and repairing cells. **5** Legal drugs, two of: tobacco, alcohol, anti-depressants, pain killers. Illegal drugs, two of: barbiturates,

heroin, amphetamines and cocaine. **6** It stops the red blood cells from carrying as much oxygen as they should, by binding to haemoglobin in the place of oxygen. **7** Ethanol. **8** Cystic fibrosis and haemophilia.

Check yourself

2.1

1 Bacterial diseases, two of: tuberculosis, salmonella, pneumonia. Viral diseases, two of: measles, rubella, flu. **2** By dividing into two. **3** By damaging cells.

2.2

1 Through cuts in the skin, the digestive, respiratory and reproductive systems, and through animal bites. **2** Condoms prevent body fluids being exchanged during sexual intercourse.

2.3

1 An antibody destroys a microorganism, whereas an anti-toxin destroys a toxin that a microorganism has produced. **2** Fragments of cells that help the blood to clot. **3** By engulfing microorganisms.

2.4

1 E.g. pasta, rice, bread. **2** For energy, growth and repair and to stay healthy. **3** Saturated fat has an animal origin, whereas unsaturated fat has a plant origin.

2.5

1 By altering the chemical reactions that take place inside your body. **2** Stimulants speed up the nervous system, whereas depressants slow down the nervous system.

2.6

1 Tar, nicotine and carbon monoxide. **2** It affects the nervous system, makes the heart beat faster and narrows blood vessels. **3** Chemicals in tobacco smoke paralyse the cilia. Mucus now flows into the lungs, making it hard to breathe and often causes infection.

2.7

1 The liver. **2** About six hours.

2.8

1 Thick sticky mucus that blocks the air passages, making it difficult to breathe and often results in chest infections. **2** A person who contains only one copy of a faulty recessive gene – they do not suffer from the disorder.

End of chapter questions

1 Using your cells. The virus invades a cell, enters the nucleus and 'tells' the nucleus to copy its genes. New viruses are made. The cell bursts and releases the new viruses, destroying your cell. **2** It is used as a store of energy, to keep you warm and cover your vital organs, protecting them from damage. **3** Somebody who is dependent on a drug. **4** Chemicals in tobacco-smoke cause alveoli walls to weaken and lose their flexibility. They do not inflate properly and can burst during coughing. Not enough oxygen passes into the blood, leaving the person breathless. **5** It is a depressant that affects your nervous system and changes your behaviour. It also damages your liver. **6** It only affects one sex.

Chapter 3

Pre Test

1 By killing the bacteria that caused the disease.
2 Washing your hands regularly, having a bath or shower daily, cleaning your teeth twice a day.
3 Dead or weakened microorgansims.
4 Electromagnetic waves of high energy.
5 Alpha, beta and gamma radiation.
6 It is swallowed or injected into the patient. The radiation emitted is detected by a gamma camera, which forms an image of the organ or system being studied. This is then analysed by doctors.

Check yourself

3.1
1 No, antibiotics only kill bacteria.
2 They reduce swelling, which in turn stops pain.

3.2
1 Worktops, toilets, sinks, hospitals.
2 Somewhere where no microorganisms are present.

3.3
1 Three of: MMR, BCG, polio, tetanus. **2** Polio

3.4
1 Bone is dense, and so absorbs the X-rays. Muscle is a soft tissue, so X-rays can pass through easily. **2** X-rays are ionising (similar to gamma rays), and so can cause cancer in humans at high exposure levels. However, they diagnose many medical conditions without the need for a surgical procedure, which carries a far higher risk of infection.

3.5
1 Alpha – paper; beta – 5 mm aluminium; gamma – thick lead. **2** Ensuring substances are handled safely; using shielding around radioactive substances; keeping exposure times as low as possible; wearing a film badge.

3.6
1 Detecting tumours, monitoring blood flow around the body or checking organs are working properly. **2** An intense beam of gamma radiation is aimed at the equipment, which is in sealed packaging.

End of chapter questions

1 Paracetamol reduces the production of prostaglandin, a chemical that makes you feel pain. **2** Both antiseptics and disinfectants kill microorganisms. However disinfectants are much stronger chemicals, they damage skin cells so must not be used on the body.
3 Vaccines contain dead or weakened microorganisms that trigger your white blood cells to make antibodies. These destroy the microorganisms. Some remain in your body and will fight the microorganism off quickly if it enters your body again, preventing it causing disease.
4 Lead absorbs X-rays well, because it is so dense. This reduces the radiation dose the radiographer receives.
5 An intense dose of radiation (either gamma from outside the body, or beta (sometimes alpha) as an implant) is aimed at the tumour. The cancer cells are killed by this radiation.

EXAMINATION-STYLE QUESTIONS

1(a) Animal cell. (1 mark)
(b) A: Cytoplasm. (1 mark)
B: Cell membrane. (1 mark)
C: Nucleus. (1 mark)
D: Mitochondria. (1 mark)
(c) Cytoplasm is a 'jelly-like' substance where all the chemical reactions take place. (1 mark)
Nucleus contains the information needed to make new cells. (1 mark)
Cell membrane is a barrier that controls what comes into and out of the cell. (1 mark)
Mitochondria – Respiration takes place here. Glucose and oxygen react and release energy. (1 mark)
(d) Cell wall. (1 mark)
Vacuole. (1 mark)
Chloroplasts. (1 mark)
2(a) In your mitochondria. (1 mark)
(b) Oxygen. (1 mark)
Water. (1 mark)
(c) Sugar **and** pasta. (1 mark)
(d) Diffusion. (1 mark)
3(a) Gamma rays. (1 mark)
Alpha particles/ beta particles. (1 mark)
X-rays. (1 mark)
Gamma rays. (1 mark)
(b) Detecting cancerous tumours / checking organs are working properly. (1 mark)
(c) Standing behind lead screen / wearing film badge / keeping exposure time as low as possible. (1 mark)
(d) One of these statements: (2 marks)
Lead screen – absorbs X-rays therefore minimising received dose.
Wearing film badge – checks exposure levels so a large dose is not received over time.
Keeping exposure times as low as possible – exposure to X-rays limited so a large dose is not received.
4(a) Haemophilia / Sickle cell anaemia / Huntington's chorea (1 mark)
(b) Carrier. (1 mark)
(c) Recessive. (1 mark)
(d) Lucy – carrier   Peter – carrier
      Cc   Cc
(1 mark)

Eggs contain: C   c
       Sperm contain: C   c   (1 mark)

During fertilisation	C	c
C	CC	Cc
c	Cc	cc

(1 mark)

Children would be born in the ratio of
1CC : 2Cc : 1cc (1 mark)
1 normal: 2 carriers: 1 cystic fibrosis
(Instead of a ratio, the likelihood of being a cystic fibrosis sufferer could be expressed in percentages. 25% likelihood of suffering from cystic fibrosis.)

Chapter 4

Pre Test

1 carbon dioxide + water → sugar + oxygen
2 Through stomata. **3** The soil. **4** Making chlorophyll. **5** A technique that produces as much food as possible, by making the best use of land, plants and animals. **6** Fertilisers, herbicides, pesticides and fungicides.

7 By adding manure or compost, or planting leguminous plants like clover, because they add nitrates to the soil. **8** Using ladybirds to eat aphids, etc.

Check yourself

4.1
1 An organism that makes its own food.
2 Xylem vessels. **3** To absorb light energy from the Sun.

4.2
1 Younger leaves would have a purple tinge and the plants would have poor root growth.
2 To release energy, as a store and to make cellulose (needed to make cell walls) and proteins (needed for growth and repair).

4.3
1 Pesticides kill pests, whereas herbicides kill weeds.
2 So that animals increase in size as quickly as possible, because they don't waste energy moving, keeping warm etc. **3** To prevent them getting diseases.

4.4
1 By using biological control techniques.
2 They have as much space as possible to roam in, shelter is provided, medical treatment is only given if an animal is unwell, and they are fed an organic diet.

End of chapter questions

1 By osmosis. **2** Light intensity, carbon dioxide concentration, water availability and temperature.
3 Healthy growth and making DNA and amino acids.
4 Using fertilisers. **5** A chemical that kills fungi.
6 So that it uses all of its energy for growth.
7 A farming technique that uses natural methods of producing crops and rearing animals. Artificial chemicals are not used and animals roam as freely as possible. **8** They remove weeds by hand or using a machine.

Chapter 5

Pre Test

1 Animal skin (usually cow). **2** The rainforest.
3 glucose → ethanol + carbon dioxide **4** Yeast.
5 By fermenting lactose (milk sugar). **6** It curdles the milk and restrains the growth of harmful bacteria. **7** By choosing the best bull and cow in their stock to breed, e.g. the cow that produces the most milk. **8** A high egg laying capability. **9** Altering an organism's genes to produce desired characteristics. **10** E.g. genetically modified cotton, which has a high cotton yield and pest resistance, and sheep that produce pharmaceuticals in their milk.

Check yourself

5.1
1 Three of: cotton, fruit, vegetables, paper, wooden table, etc. **2** Three of: wool, leather, meat, fur, suede, etc.
3 Three of: beer, bread, wine, yoghurt, cheese etc.

5.2
1 The ethanol evaporates when the bread is cooked.
2 A good supply of glucose, with no oxygen present, at a temperature between 15°C and 25 °C.

5.3

1 Bacteria and rennet. **2** Water.

5.4

1 A thick fleecy coat (or high milk production if the sheep are used for making cheese). **2** Animals and plants display desired characteristics, it can improve pest/frost/temperature resistance.

5.5

1 It is much quicker (one generation) and more accurate. **2** Genes that come from another organism.

End of chapter questions

1 One of: woad, onion, tumeric, etc.
2 An animal origin, it is produced by silk worms.
3 glucose → ethanol + carbon dioxide.
4 Lactose. **5** It reduces variation by reducing the number of genes (the gene pool) from which a species is created. **6** At a very early (normally embryonic) stage.

Chapter 6

Pre Test

1 Elements contain only one type of atom, compounds are different atoms joined together, mixtures can contain different elements and compounds that are not chemically joined together. Mixtures can be easily separated.
2 Compound. **3** Limestone, gold, sulfur, marble.
4 Crude oil. **5** Carbon, hydrogen and oxygen.
6 Four. **7** A substance taken from the ground that contains enough metal compounds to be worth extracting. **8** A chemical that is used to extract metals from metal oxides. **9** Increased income, jobs being created. **10** Global warming, acid rain, toxic chemicals from mine site, damage to landscape.

Check yourself
6.1

1 A compound. **2** The third picture (a mixture).
3 Mixtures are not joined together chemically.

6.2

1 Sulfur is used to make sulfuric acid. **2** Rock.
3 Different boiling points.

6.3

1 Mg, Cl, Pb. **2** Six. **3** CH_4.

6.4

1 Oxygen. **2** Coke + oxygen → carbon dioxide, Coke + carbon dioxide → carbon monoxide, Carbon monoxide + iron oxide → carbon dioxide + iron. **3** Iron: carbon monoxide, lead: carbon.

6.5

1 Resources are needed for industry, resources can be sold, jobs are created. **2** (a) Toxic chemicals leeching into soil, damage to the landscape. (b) Global warming from CO_2 emissions, acid rain from increased traffic.
3 Sustainability – managing industry to minimum damage to the environment. Stakeholder – someone affected by decisions made by others, i.e. mining operators.

End of chapter questions

1 Oxygen molecule – two identical oxygen atoms bonded together. Carbon dioxide molecule – two oxygen atoms bonded to a carbon atom. Carbon dioxide is a compound because it contains two types of atom.

2 Crude oil is used to produce fuels, plastics, tar, paints and medicines. The different hydrocarbons are separated by fractional distillation. **3** NH_3.
4 See diagram on p.38. **5** Damage to the local landscape. Toxic chemicals from mine polluting area. Traffic increasing. Safety for children.

Chapter 7

Pre Test

1 Coal takes millions of years to form – we haven't got the time to make more.
2

Heat energy from fuel	→	Heat energy of steam	→	Kinetic energy of turbine blades	→	Electrical energy is generated

3 Examples could include anti-freeze, medicines, paints, plastics, solvents, cosmetics, petrol, diesel, propane, butane, fuel oils, lubricants, road asphalt, insulation. **4** No, nuclear power is not a renewable resource as there is only a limited amount of suitable uranium available for use as a fuel. **5** Three of: solar, wind, wave, HEP, biomass and geothermal energy.

Check yourself
7.1

1 Eg wood or alcohol (ethanol). **2** The main problem is that they are our major energy resources and will get more and more expensive as they run out, until there is no more left for us to use.

7.2

1 As the water enters the power station, it passes into pipes that run through the furnace, where it gets heated up and turns to steam. As steam, it passes into the turbine, where its energy makes the huge blades spin. It leaves the power station as cooler steam through the cooling towers. **2** A million 100 W light bulbs could be lit by a 100 MW power station.

7.3

1 Carbon monoxide and NOx could damage your health. **2** If we recycle our plastics more, we will need to use less crude oil to make plastics and so free it up for other uses.

7.4

1 Arguments should include that the wastes it produces are dangerously radioactive and that it is a non-renewable resource and so will not be a long-term solution to the problem. **2** A nuclear power station produces none of the pollution gases that fossil fuel power stations do – but they do produce radioactive wastes that are expensive and dangerous to dispose of.

7.5

1 Most of our energy comes from non-renewable resources and these will run out. If we can't develop renewable resources, we will run out of cheap energy and will not be able to use as much as we do. Also, burning less fossil fuel will help combat global warming. **2** When you think about which resources you could use, you need to think about their advantages and disadvantages – which could provide you with reliable, regular energy at an affordable price? **3** Biomass is a fuel – so it combusts in oxygen to produce carbon dioxide and other polluting gases. None of the other alternative fuels combust.

End of chapter questions

1 Coal was formed from the remains of plants that grew in the Carboniferous Period, about 300 million years ago. The energy for these living plants that came from the Sun was stored in them as chemical energy and has stayed there across the millions of years it took for the plants to become fossils. **2** Every time energy is transferred from one form to another in a power station, some is wasted (often as heat). Because there are several energy transfers in the station, there are many opportunities for energy loss.
3 Fossil fuels are non-renewable and so will run out. They cause pollution when they are burned.
4 Arguments for nuclear power should include that it produces no pollution gases, is no more expensive than coal and will last for decades longer than oil and gas will. **5** Biofuels are most easily available – from crops, as well as from waste. Also, they can be burnt to produce reliable energy on demand.

EXAMINATION-STYLE QUESTIONS

1 (a) Three marks for all correct. One mark for only one right:
Furnace – This is where the fuel is burnt to release heat energy.
Turbine – These blades are made to spin by the steam.
Generator – When this spins, it makes electricity. (3 marks)
(b) (i) Renewable. (1 mark)
(ii) Coal. (1 mark)
(iii) Solar. (1 mark)
(c) Oil, carbon, wind. (3 marks)
2 (a) Fossil. (1 mark)
(b) Millions. (1 mark)
(c) Wave, wind. (2 marks)
(d) Fossil fuels all produce pollution – we need to find energy sources that don't. (1 mark)
3 (a) Fertiliser gives the plants the nutrients it needs to grow effectively. (1 mark)
Herbicide kills weeds. (1 mark)
Fungicide kills fungi. (1 mark)
Pesticide kills pests. (1 mark)
(b) Temperature and diet. (2 marks)
(c) All the animal's energy is used for growth, and is not wasted moving around. (1 mark)
4 (a) Selective breeding. (1 mark)
(b) It reduces the gene pool / variation within a species. (1 mark)
(c) It is much quicker – occurs in one generation. (1 mark)
It is more accurate – desired characteristics can be chosen. (1 mark)
(d) The insulin gene is removed from the nucleus of a human cell. (1 mark)
The foreign gene is then put into a circular piece of DNA called a plasmid. (This is known as recombinant DNA.) (1 mark)
The recombinant DNA / plasmid is put into a bacterial cell. (1 mark)
The bacteria reproduce lots of times, producing lots of copies of the recombinant DNA / plasmid. (1 mark)
The bacteria produce large quantities of insulin, which is extracted and purified for medical use. (1 mark)
5 (a) Advantages, up to two from:
Society needs materials for building and other uses.

Materials can be sold.
Mining creates jobs. (2 marks)
Harms the environment, up to two from:
Poisonous chemicals can be washed into rivers and lakes.
Spoils the landscape.
Processing ores produces carbon dioxide, which adds to global warming.
Increased traffic to and from mine increases pollution levels. (2 marks)
(b) Balancing social need with environmental harm. (1 mark)
Monitoring and trying to reduce pollutant levels. (1 mark)
Involving stakeholders in decisions. (1 mark)

Chapter 8

Pre Test
1 (a) Negative. (b) Positive. 2 Atoms are the individual particles that bond together to make molecules. 3 A charged particle. 4 Their atoms share electrons that are free to move. 5 Brittle. 6 When atoms share their electrons. 7 Ionic. 8 Sodium – positive, chloride – negative. 9 Weak forces holding the molecules together. 10 Diamond and graphite.

Check yourself
8.1
1 Protons and neutrons. 2 Neutral. 3 Six.
8.2
1 An oxygen molecule is two oxygen atoms bonded together. 2 Positive.
8.3
1 (Check this answer on a periodic table.) 2 See diagram on p.48. 3 Metals, three of: high melting and boiling points, strong, dense, shiny, malleable, ductile, conductors. Non-metals, three of: low melting and boiling points, not dense, dull, brittle, insulators.
8.4
1 Carbon dioxide. 2 X. 3 Share.
8.5
1 Sodium chloride. 2 Y. 3 Transferred.
8.6
1 Diamond – covalent bonding. Sodium chloride – ionic bonding. 2 The atoms are held in position by very strong forces.

End of chapter questions
1 Proton – positive charge, mass of 1, in the nucleus. Neutron – no charge, mass of 1, in the nucleus. Electron – negative charge, almost no mass, orbits the nucleus. 2 Left-hand side. 3 They are malleable – their shared electrons allow the atoms to slip over each other. 4 It contains non-metal atoms and has a low boiling point. 5 Crystal. 6 Three of: diamond, graphite, sodium chloride, silica.

Chapter 9

Pre Test
1 Calcium carbonate. 2 By heating limestone. 3 By roasting quicklime with clay and gypsum. 4 Sand. 5 Concrete contains small rocks and stones. 6 They are ductile and good electrical conductors. 7 Can be bent or hammered into shape. 8 A combination of different materials. 9 In the kitchen and bathroom. 10 Three of: low density, insulators, flexible, weak.

Check yourself
9.1
1 Three of: cement, paper, steel, glass. 2 Limestone – calcium carbonate. Quicklime – calcium oxide. Slaked lime – calcium hydroxide. 3 $CaCO_3$.
9.2
1 Producing cement and neutralising acid rain. 2 Quicklime + water → slaked lime 3 It requires energy to take place.
9.3
1 Limestone is heated to produce quicklime. Quicklime is roasted with clay and gypsum to produce cement. Cement is mixed with water and sand to produce mortar. 2 Cement, sand, water and small stones. 3 Sand and sodium carbonate.
9.4
1 They are electrical conductors. 2 They are malleable. 3 They are not brittle.
9.5
1 High melting point and poor conductors of heat. 2 Light, can be moulded into shape. 3 Fibres of glass within a polymer resin.
9.6
1 Own answer. 2 The wires stop the glass from shattering, because they are not brittle. 3 Glass – attractive and easy to clean, but brittle. Wood – cheap, easy to cut into shape, light, but can be scratched or stained. Metal – hard and strong, can be made into shape, but very dense and heavy. Polymer – light, cheap and can be moulded into shape, but not very strong.

End of chapter questions
1 Two of: glass, mortar, concrete. 2 Exothermic. 3 Concrete. 4 Malleability. 5 Ceramics. 6 Cheap, light, can be moulded into shape.

Chapter 10

Pre Test
1 Examples could include: torch – batteries, gas cooker, coal/wood fire, anything plugged into the electricity.
2 power = voltage × current = $230 \times 6 = 1380W$
3 Normally, the fuse allows the right amount of current to flow through it. But if too much current flows, the wire in the fuse overheats and melts, breaking the circuit.
4 energy = power x time = $2kW \times 4$ hours = 8kWh
5 Conduction – heat flows through a solid by passing along vibration energy. Convection – warm fluids rise and take the heat with them. Radiation – infra-red radiation is given out from anything warm and can even travel through empty space.
6 $efficiency = \dfrac{\text{useful energy output}}{\text{total energy output}}$ (× 100 to get a %)
7 Because more efficient devices will be cheaper to run and will make our energy resources last longer.

Check yourself
10.1
1 For example, gas, electricity, wood. 2 Electrical lighting is easier to start (by just switching it on) and is safer because it is not flammable. 3 Some rural areas don't have reliable gas or electricity supplies, so they keep a tank of fuel oil to burn and generate heat and electricity.
10.2
1 energy = power x time = $1200W \times (3 \times 60)s$ = 216000J (= 216kJ) 2 current = power ÷ voltage = $60 \div 230 = 0.26A$ 3 Energy is measured in joules, power in watts, voltage in volts and current in amperes (amps).
10.3
1 When too much current flows through the circuit beaker, an electromagnet operates a switch to turn off the circuit until the fault that caused the problem is fixed. 2 power = voltage × current = $230 \times 6 = 1380W$ 3 (a) It will work because it will allow current to flow in the circuit again. (b) It will allow too much current to flow and will not blow, possibly causing a fire from overheating wires.
10.4
1 First: energy = power x time = $60 \times (60 \times 60)$ = 216000J (= 216kJ)
Second: energy = $100 \times (45 \times 60) = 270000J$ (= 270kJ) So the 100W bulb uses more.
2 (a) $60 \times 60 = 3600s$ (b) 1000 (c) $3600 \times 1000 = 3600000J$ in a kWh
10.5
1 By conduction – which is different to in fluids because the particles are fixed in place and cannot move to take the energy with them. 2 The foil reflects the infra-red radiation back into the room, to stop it being lost.
3 (a) The air gap means that heat cannot conduct to the outside. (b) The air is sealed in at the top, so any air in the gap that gets warmed cannot rise and leave the window.
10.6
1 The diagram should show electrical energy as the input, sound and light as useful output energies and heat as a waste energy.
2 efficiency = useful output / total input = (500–400) / 500 = 0.2 (or × 100 = 20 %)
10.7
1 Because energy efficient light bulbs use less energy when they work and last longer – so save you money in the longer run. 2 The energy efficient light bulb wastes 65 J every second. The filament bulb wastes 90 J every second. 3 The lid on the saucepan prevents heat from being lost, so it stays in the pan to cook more quickly and so less is used.

End of chapter questions
1 Batteries are portable and safe to use anywhere. 2 A stereo transfers electricity to sound and will waste heat. 3 current = power ÷ voltage = $1500 \div 230 = 6.5A$ so a 10A fuse would be best. 4 energy = power × time = $1.5kW \times 3h = 4.5$ kWh. Cost = $4.5 \times 7 = 32.5$ p a day. 5 Loft insulation reduces convection in the loft space because it stops the air getting warmed by conduction through the ceilings beneath it. 6 The diagram should show electrical energy being turned to useful light (about 10 %) and waste heat (about 90 %). 7 Suggestions could include only having the part with bread in getting hot, reflective surfaces behind the heating element could reflect the heat back in; maybe there is a way that the convection losses could be reduced by putting a lid on it.

Chapter 11

Pre Test

1 Solution, suspension, aerosol, gel, foam, emulsion.
2 **Solute** – substance dissolved in a solvent. **Solution** – a mixture of solvent and solute. **Soluble** – able to dissolve in a solvent. **Solvent** – substance able to dissolve a solute. 3 Gel.
4 They are immiscible. 5 Solutions, suspensions, gels.

Check yourself

11.1

1 Solution. 2 Foam. 3 Aerosol.

11.2

1 Soluble aspirin, toothpaste, shaving foam, hair gel, mayonnaise. 2 Soluble aspirin, toothpaste, shaving foam, hair gel, deodorant spray.

11.3

1 Water molecules collide with the surface of the solid solute. The water molecules can disrupt the solid structure of the solute. The solute starts to come apart. The solute particles end up evenly spaced throughout the solution. 2 They can be poisonous, cause chemical burns or even cancer. 3 The paint would dissolve in the rain.

11.4

1 Filtration. 2 To spread the medicine out evenly through the mixture. 3 Chromatography.

End of chapter questions

1 A solution is solid particles dissolved in a liquid, but a gel is a liquid trapped in a solid framework.
2 One of: mayonnaise, chocolate. 3 Ethanol, acetone, white spirit. (Organic solvents)
4 Evaporate the water.

EXAMINATION-STYLE QUESTIONS

1 (a) Limestone – calcium carbonate, $CaCO_3$
     (2 marks)
   Quicklime – calcium oxide, CaO (2 marks)
   Slaked lime – calcium hydroxide, $Ca(OH)_2$
     (2 marks)
  (b) (i) It takes in energy from its surroundings.
     (1 mark)
     (ii) Carbon dioxide. (1 mark)
2 (a) Malleability. (1 mark)
  (b) Metals have closely packed atoms surrounded by free electrons. (1 mark)
   The atoms can slide over each other when pushed. (1 mark)
  (c) Iron. (1 mark)
3 (a) Four of: insulators, strong, hard, resistant to chemicals, high melting point. (4 marks)
  (b) Insulating, so not cold to the touch. (1 mark)
   Strong, so won't break easily. (1 mark)
   Hard, so won't get scratched or worn away. (1 mark)
   Resistant to chemicals, so won't be damaged by toilet cleaners. (1 mark)
4 (a) Immiscible liquids. (2 marks)
  (b) Helps the liquids mix. (1 mark)
  (c) You can see two layers of liquid. (1 mark)
5 (a) Suspension. (1 mark)
  (b) So the concentration of medicine is the same throughout the mixture. (1 mark)
  (c) A=chromatography, B=filtration, C=evaporation, D=distillation, E=sieving.
     (5 marks)

6 (a) (i) Filament.
     (ii) Energy efficient.
     (iii) Filament.
     (iv) Energy efficient. (4 marks)
  (b) (i) power = energy ÷ time (1 mark)
     (ii) energy = power × time = 100 × (60 × 60) = 360 000 J (360 kJ) (2 marks)
     (iii) energy used usefully = 10 % of 360 000 J = 36 000 J, so energy wasted = 90 % of this = 324 000 J (324 kJ) (3 marks)

Chapter 12

Pre Test

1 speed = distance ÷ time = 500 ÷ 20 = 25 m/s 2 distance = velocity × time = 15 × 60 = 900 m 3 acceleration = change in velocity ÷ time taken = 30 ÷ 15 = 2 m/s² 4 time = change in velocity ÷ acceleration = 24 ÷ 1.5 = 16 s 5 'Thinking distance' is the distance travelled between seeing a problem and hitting the brakes. 'Braking distance' is the distance travelled between hitting the brakes and stopping. 6 Icy or wet road, poor brakes, worn tyres. 7 Using a mobile phone takes your attention away from your driving – and occupies one of your hands too, if you aren't using a hands-free kit. 8 In built up areas, there are many more reasons why you might need to stop suddenly – and you can also see less far ahead in built up areas, so need to be able to stop in a shorter distance.

Check yourself

12.1

1 speed = distance ÷ time = 100 ÷ 5 = 20 m/s
2 distance = speed x time = 15 × (5 × 60) = 4500 m (4.5 km)

12.2

1 units for distance = metres, time = seconds, velocity = metres per second and acceleration = metres per second squared 2 acceleration = change in velocity ÷ time taken = 9 ÷ 2 = 4.5 m/s²

12.3

1 For example, if it is fast, has poor brakes and worn tyres, the road is slippery and the driver is tired and on the phone. 2 (a) You need to leave enough distance in front of you to stop in time. (b) If you are travelling faster, your stopping distance is increased and so you need to leave a larger gap in which to stop.

12.4

1 (a) Make sure his speed is close to, but not over 40 m.p.h. (b) Be alert and prepared to stop if she sees pedestrians crossing. (c) Slow down in preparation for a sharp left bend. (d) Slow and be alert for patches of slippery road. 2 Eating or drinking takes your attention away from your driving – and occupies one of your hands too, which means you have less control.

End of chapter questions

1 time = distance ÷ velocity = 5000 ÷ 25 = 200 s 2 velocity = distance ÷ time = (600 × 1000) ÷ (60 × 60) = 167 m/s 3 acceleration = change in velocity ÷ time taken = 10 ÷ 2.5 = 4 m/s² 4 change in velocity = acceleration × time taken = 5 × 7 = 35 m/s 5 Thinking distance increases because you travel further in your reaction time. Braking distance increases because it takes longer for the brakes to remove

all of the kinetic energy. 6 Tiredness, distraction (e.g. using a phone), drinking alcohol.
7 Because drunk drivers have a longer reaction time, as well as being easily distracted from their driving. 8 If the brakes and tyres have worn down, then there will be less friction and so the car will take longer to stop – and may also skid out of control.

Chapter 13

Pre Test

1 hydrocarbon + oxygen → carbon dioxide + water 2 efficiency = (660 / 2000) × 100 = 33% 3 Harmless: water, carbon dioxide. Harmful: carbon monoxide, VOCs, NO_x. 4 Alcohol is a renewable fuel and can burn cleanly.

Check yourself

13.1

1 Carbon dioxide and water (vapour). 2 Petrol (gasoline) and diesel. 3 Longer hydrocarbon chains can release more energy when burnt.

13.2

1 To make cars that use (or waste) less energy and to make less pollution. 2 500 × (40 / 30) = 667 km. So extra distance = 667 – 500 = 167 km further.

13.3

1 When complete combustion happens, there is enough oxygen for all of the hydrogen and carbon in the hydrocarbon fuel to react with. With incomplete combustion, there isn't enough oxygen to fully react, so more pollution is created, e.g. carbon monoxide. 2 Problems such as smog, acid rain, asthma, ozone layer depletion.
3 A catalytic converter reduces harmful emissions in a number of ways, e.g. by splitting up NO_x into harmless nitrogen and oxygen gases, and by adding oxygen to carbon monoxide to produce carbon dioxide.

13.4

1 Petrol and diesel are non-renewable and cause pollution when they combust. We are looking for alternative fuels that are renewable and cause less pollution. 2 Electric cars cause very little pollution and can be recharged from renewable sources (e.g. solar- or wind-generated electricity), but the battery packs are large and heavy and need frequent recharging. 3 While using LPG is a good idea because it will allow our petrol and diesel to last longer, it still comes from crude oil, which is non-renewable, so our sources of LPGs will run out too.

End of chapter questions

1 $CH_4 + 2O_2 \rightarrow CO_2 + 2H_2O$ 2 Three of: fuel gas, LPG (liquid petroleum gases – propane and butane); petrol, gasoline – car fuel; naphtha – not a fuel, but can be broken down to make fuels; paraffin, kerosene – used as domestic heater fuel, jet fuel; diesel oil, gas oil – used by some cars and larger vehicles; fuel oils and waxes – central heating oil, candles. 3 Engines generate a lot of heat as the fuel combusts – a lot of this heat makes the engine itself hot, as well as heating up the air around it or being lost through the exhaust. An engine also wastes a lot of energy as sound.
4 An 'emissions test' detects when an engine is putting out too much pollution, such as NOx or carbon monoxide. If this is detected in test, then the problem can be sorted out.

Chapter 14

Pre Test

1 Radiowaves, microwaves, infra-red, visible, ultra-violet, X-rays, gamma rays.   **2** For medium range communication, e.g. mobile phones and satellites.

3 (a) X-ray images can help diagnose broken bones.
(b) High doses of X-rays can damage cells and cause cancers.   **4** Some microwave frequencies are used for cooking. Although these are different to those used in communication, there are still some fears that these may cause damage through heating.   **5** Astronomers use radio telescopes to search for extra-terrestrial life, as well as for low energy emissions from distant objects.

6 Most scientists think the Universe began with a 'Big Bang': a large explosion, from which everything is still flying outwards.

Check yourself

14.1

1 (a) Radio has the longest wavelength. (b) Gamma has the highest frequency. (c) Gamma has the most energy. (d) Both travel at the same speed.   **2** Energy is in joules, wavelength in metres, frequency in Hertz and wave speed in metres per second.

14.2

1 Radio waves are used to transmit information over long distances. They are also used in radar systems to detect objects.   **2** Infra-red radiation is given off by anything warm. Police and military use goggles or cameras that detect the IR in the dark and turn it into visible light that can be seen.

14.3 / 14.4

1 A shiny mirror reflects visible light, a matt black surface absorbs it and a transparent one, like glass, transmits it.   **2** X-rays and microwaves both travel at the same speed. X-rays have a shorter wavelength, but higher frequency and energy **3** Writing in it on your property only shows up when UV is shone on it.   **4** (a) Proportional. (b) Inversely proportional. (c) Inversely proportional.   **5** Strongly focussed gamma rays will kill cancer cells. But gamma rays can sometimes also damage healthy cells and cause cancers.

14.5

1 The ultra-violet light from the Sun is what causes skin tanning (and skin cancers). We can feel the infra-red radiation from the Sun as warmth.
2 (a) 9 planets (but there are more in other Solar Systems). (b) 1 star (our Sun). (c) 0 galaxies (we are in a galaxy, called the Milky Way).   **3** Neither gamma rays nor radio waves can be focussed by the lenses and mirrors in normal 'optical' telescopes – and they wouldn't be visible to our human eyes anyway.

14.6

1 (a) Galactic red-shift is evidence that the Universe is expanding, as wavelengths given out by objects moving away shift towards the red end of the spectrum. (b) Cosmic microwave background radiation is 'left over' heat from the explosion.   **2** Red-shift could be detected with an optical telescope, as the visible light from stars shifts towards the red, and microwave background with a radio telescope as microwave radiation behaves a lot like short radio waves.

End of chapter questions

1 Radio waves, microwaves, infra-red, visible, ultra-violet, X-rays, gamma rays.   **2** Light reflects from the inside of the fibre and so bounces all the way along.

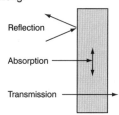

Reflection

Absorption

Transmission

3 (a) Gamma rays can be used to sterilise food and equipment. (b) They can also burn skin and damage cells.   **4** Infra-red rays come from the hot surface of Venus – and radio waves (radar) that we send in through the clouds can bounce back to us.   **5** The red-shift of light from distant galaxies tells us that they are all heading away from us, i.e. that the Universe is expanding.

1 (a) (i) Cars with higher acceleration have higher top speeds. (1 mark)
(ii) The Ford Puma. (1 mark)
(iii) Estimates should be about 180 m.p.h. (175–182 km/h). (1 mark)
(iv) Distance = speed × time = 185 × 0.5
= 92.5 km (3 marks)
(b) (i) Acceleration = change in speed / time for change = 27/13.5 = 2 m/s² (3 marks)
(ii) The Vauxhall Astra is the most efficient of these cars, because it has the highest fuel consumption, meaning it travels the furthest for an amount of petrol. (2 marks)

2 (a) (i) Renewable means that the resource will not run out because it can be replaced. (1 mark)
(ii) Because fossil fuels will run out and we also need cleaner energy resources. (2 marks)
(b) (i) Hydroelectric. (1 mark)
(ii) Landfill gas. (1 mark)
(iii) Pollution, when burned it will release carbon dioxide and other gases. (2 marks)
(c) Both are free environmental resources and unreliable / not available all of the time. (2 marks)

3 (a) Copy of table on p.84.
Energy of wave column: Low, Medium, High (2 marks)

Transmitted or absorbed by atmosphere column: Transmitted, Absorbed (2 marks)
Where detectors / telescopes can be: Ground, Satellite (2 marks)
(b) (i) Ultra-violet (allow X-rays because some UV does get through). (1 mark)
(ii) The IR gets more difficult to detect the deeper they travel into the atmosphere. At the top of mountains they haven't got too weak and so can still be detected. (1 mark)
(c) Satellites are very expensive to build and launch – and extremely expensive to repair if something goes wrong. (2 marks)

Paper 1

1 (a) Nicotine is addictive. (1 mark)
Tar causes cancer. (1 mark)
Carbon monoxide reduces the amount of
oxygen the blood can carry. (1 mark)
(b) A chemical that alters the way the body
works. (1 mark)
(c) Nervous system. (1 mark)
(d) Withdrawal symptoms. (1 mark)
2 (a) 0.1 g (1 mark)
(b) 15 g (1 mark)
(c) Fat. (1 mark)
Carbohydrate. (1 mark)
Protein. (1 mark)
(d) It sticks to the lining of your blood vessels.
(1 mark)
This makes them narrower. (1 mark)
Your heart has to work harder to pump the
blood through these vessels, which
increases your risk of a heart attack. (1 mark)
3 (a) Yeast – bread, wine. (1 mark)
Bacteria – cheese, yoghurt. (1 mark)
(b) Fermentation. (1 mark)
(c) Carbon dioxide. (1 mark)
(d) Milk is boiled. / Bacteria are added. (1 mark)
Milk is kept warm for several hours allowing
the bacteria to multiply. (1 mark)
Bacteria ferment lactose into lactic acid.
(1 mark)
The lactic acid produced curdles the
milk into yoghurt. (1 mark)
4 (a) Droplet infection. (1 mark)
Condoms. (1 mark)
HIV / hepatitis. (Accept other blood-
transmitted diseases.) (1 mark)
(b) Measles / mumps / rubella / polio / tetanus /
tuberculosis / diphtheria. (1 mark)
(c) The microorganisms are dead or weakened.
(1 mark)
(d) The microorganisms in the vaccine trigger
your white blood cells to make antibodies.
(1 mark)
The antibodies destroy the microorganisms.
(1 mark)
Some antibodies remain in your body and
will fight the microorganism off quickly if it
enters your body again. (1 mark)

Paper 2

1 (a)

Name	Molecular formula	Boiling point (°C)	State at 25°C
methane	CH_4	–164	gas
ethane	C_2H_6	–89	**gas**
propane	C_3H_8	–42	**gas**
butane	C_4H_{10}	–0.5	**gas**
pentane	C_5H_{12}	36	liquid
hexane	C_6H_{14}	69	**liquid**

(3 marks)
(b) C is carbon, H is hydrogen. (2 marks)
(c) (i) (Complete) combustion. (1 mark)
(ii) Carbon dioxide and water. (2 marks)
(d) Hexane releases the most energy when it is
burned, because it has the most carbon
atoms (which will release more energy when
reacting with oxygen). (2 marks)
2 (a) (i) 'Thinking distance' is the distance
travelled between seeing a problem and
hitting the brakes. 'Braking distance' is
the distance travelled between hitting the
brakes and stopping. (2 marks)
(ii) 20 + 75 = 95 m (1 mark)
(b) (i) speed = distance travelled ÷ time taken.
(1 mark)
(ii) time taken = distance travelled ÷ speed
= 20 ÷ 30 = 0.67 s (2 marks)
(c) (i) acceleration = change in speed ÷
time taken. (1 mark)
(ii) acceleration = change in speed ÷ time
taken = (0 – 30) ÷ 5 = (-) 6 m/s² (2 marks)
3 (a) Copy of table on p.87.
(i) m / s (1 mark)
(ii) Across a field, Across the Solar System,
Around the world (2 marks)
(iii) Megaphone, Transmitter, Microphone
(2 marks)
(b) (i) There are fears that the microwaves
produced by mobile phones might cause
a heating effect on the water (or fats) in
our heads, damaging or killing cells.
(2 marks)
(ii) Disadvantages: mobiles cost more and
can run out of charge (or credit!).
Advantages: portability / ease of contact
of mobile
phones, other features on phones
e.g. text, cameras etc. (2 marks)
4 (a) (i) If a chemical has a boiling point lower
than room temperature (about 20°C) then
it will have boiled (become a gas) before
reaching room temperature. (2 marks)
(ii) Pentane – its boiling point is higher than
room temperature (so it would still be a
liquid). (2 marks)
(b) (i) C is carbon and H is hydrogen. (2 marks)
(ii) Carbon dioxide and water. (2 marks)
(c) (i) CO (1 mark)
(ii) C (1 mark)

Paper 3

1 (a) 6 (1 mark)
(b) 1 (1 mark)
(c) Neutrons. (1 mark)
(d) (i) Positive. (ii) Negative. (2 marks)
(e) Covalent. (1 mark)
(f) Fractional distillation. (2 marks)
(g) Any two from: limestone, gold, sulfur,
marble. (2 marks)
2 (a) Compound. (1 mark)
(b) Carbon. (1 mark)
(c) They are close together. (1 mark)
(d) PbO (1 mark)
(e) Any two statements from:
Toxic chemicals being washed from the mine
into lakes and rivers could harm wildlife.
Carbon dioxide production
could lead to more global warming.
Increased traffic around mine will add
to global warming and acid rain. (4 marks)
3 (a) Glass is transparent (1 mark)
so it's suitable for windows. (1 mark)
Metal is malleable (1 mark)
so it will bend when hit and not shatter.
(1 mark)
(b) Fibreglass. (1 mark)
4 (a) Powdered flu remedy – solute.
Hot water – solvent.
Flu remedy drink – solution. (3 marks)
(b) Water is able to get between the particles of
flu remedy and break them apart. (2 marks)
(c) Evaporate the water to leave behind the flu
remedy. (2 marks)